Robert Edward

The Doxology Approven

The singing Glory to the Father, Son and Holy Ghost in the worship of God, its lawfulness and expediency proven from the Holy Scriptures, councils and Fathers, and the scruples of the weak thereanent, cleared

Robert Edward

The Doxology Approven
The singing Glory to the Father, Son and Holy Ghost in the worship of God, its lawfulness and expediency proven from the Holy Scriptures, councils and Fathers, and the scruples of the weak thereanent, cleared

ISBN/EAN: 9783337291563

Printed in Europe, USA, Canada, Australia, Japan

Cover: Foto ©Lupo / pixelio.de

More available books at **www.hansebooks.com**

THE
DOXOLOGY
Approven:

OR,
The singing Glory to the Father, Son and Holy Ghost in the Worship of GOD, Its lawfulness and expediency proven from the Holy Scriptures, Councils and Fathers, and the Scruples of the Weak thereanent, cleared.

BY
Mr. ROBERT EDWARD,
Minister of the Gospel of Christ at *Murrois*.

Καὶ σοὶ τὴν δόξαν καὶ εὐχαριςίαν καὶ προσκύνησιν ἀναπέμπομεν. Τῶ πατρὶ καὶ τῶ υἱῶ καὶ τῶ ἁγίω πνεύματι νῦν, καὶ ἀεὶ καὶ εἰς τὲς αἰῶνας τῶν αἰώνων. *St. Basil in Liturgia.* Δόξα τῶ πατρὶ καὶ τῶ υἱῶ, καὶ τῶ ἁγίω πνεύματι, νῦν καὶ ἀεὶ, καὶ εἰς τὲς αἰῶνας τῶν αἰώνων, ἀμήν. *St. Chrysostomus in Lyturgia.*

1 Cor. 11. 16. Quod si quis videtur contentiosus esse, nos ejusmodi consuetudinem non habemus, neque Ecclesiæ Dei ——— Doxologiam respuere.

Rom. 15. 5, 6. *Now the God of patience and consolation, grant you to be like-minded one towards another, according to Christ Jesus: That ye may with one mind and one mouth glorifie God, even the Father of our Lord Jesus Christ.*

EDINBURGH,
Printed by the Heir of *Andrew Anderson*, Printer to the King's most Sacred Majesty, Anno DOMINI, M. DC. LXXXIII.

To the Right Honourable
GEORGE
Earl of Aberdene,
Viscount of Farmertin, Lord HADDO, METHLICK, TARVES and KELLE; Sheriff principal of *Edinburgh* and *Aberdene*:

Lord High - Chancellor
OF
SCOTLAND.

My Lord,

Whatsoever Maxim relating to Religion, albeit it be neither Fundamental nor Orthodox, yet these Persons who are entangled in Errour, and Slaves to their Corruption; if they fancy that Maxim to be both Fundamental and Orthodox, close

The Epistle Dedicatory.

close with it in their Judgment, embrace it in their Will, and dandle it upon the knees of their Affections; yea, they idolize it as fondly and furiously as these Pagan *Ephesians* did their Image of *Diana*, *Acts* 19. 34, 35. which they strongly believed fell down from *Jupiter*; yea, often they lay all the stress of their Religion upon that their Opinion, and will concenter with none in Love, but with these that will concenter with them in their Judgment, and cry up their great *Diana* with them; nay, they are so transported with their Fancy, that their Idol-Maxim is esteemed by them one of the noble Parts, and lies so near to the Heart of Religion, that there is no Salvation but in that way of theirs; albeit it were a Path never beaten before, and far from the true Old Way: wherefore they think they are obliged in Conscience to seperate, and keep no Church-fellowship with these that are not of their Judgment; hence a Schism and Separation in Worship, flowing from Separation in Affection, and that from Separation in Judgment, and when once Altar is reared up against Altar, follows Sword against Sword, and Camp against Camp, Division and Schism in the Church, begetting Sedition in the State: Therefore St. *Paul*, among the wicked works of the Flesh, *Gal.* 5. 19. hath coupled Seditions and Heresies together. This sad truth is known to the Learned, by many Histories in many Kingdoms; and of the strong affinity betwixt Schism and Sedition,

The Epistle Dedicatory.

dition, St. *Basil* writes most pithily; *Hippocrates* Twins were so near of Nature, that always when the one was sick the other also; but Church and State are of a nearer union, for these same Persons both for Souls and Bodies are Subjects and Servants to God in Christ, united by the same Faith and Worship, in relation to Eternal Happiness, and Subjects also to one and the same King on Earth, united by the same Laws, in relation to their civil and external Well-being; and as the Spiritual Concernment and Eternal Salvation of that Body will more affect it then its short and external Well-being on Earth, so any Member in that Body disjoynted, in regard of Spiritual-union, will cause such a stir and trouble, as during the time of its dislocation, the whole Body will be so tormented, that no civil Bonds will prevail to compose them: They will brag to sacrifise their Temporal Life, for their Eternal Salvation; *hence ariseth debates, envyings, wraths, strifes, backbitings, whisperings, swellings, tumults*, 2 Cor. 12. 20. *then confusion and every evil work*, James 3. 16.

Ἐχθρας ἀρκετὰ πρόφασις τὸ μὴ συμβῆναι ταῖς δόξαις. πάσης δὲ συν ἀμοιβίας πιστότερον πρὸς κοινωνίαν στάσεως ἡ τοῦ σφάλματ[ος] ὁμοίοτης, Basil Tom. 2. lib. de Spiritu Sancto contra eunomium Arianum, cap. 30. *Sufficiens est inimicitiæ causa opinionibus dissentire & erroris similitudo, res est quavis conjuratione fidelior ad seditionis societatem.*

Wherefore as a compassionate Member of the Mystical Body of Jesus, the least of the sons of *Levi*, whom the Holy Ghost hath made Overseer of

The Epistle Dedicatory.

of a part of the Flock of God, I have written this little Treatise for information of the Judgment of the weak Lambs of the chief Shepherd, who being unskilful in the word of Righteousness, refuse to sing the *Doxology,* because of their Doubts and Scruples, which by this Treatise, through the help of God, I have endeavoured to remove, that there be no longer division in Judgment, Affection and Worship, upon that account.

My Lord, All the Miseries and Confusions in this Land, (more than fourty Years continuance,) began at *Schism* in the Church, which is well known by sad experience, and its Tragical History is written with red Capital Letters of Blood, that he who runs may read it; with the blood of his Royal Majesty, now a glorified Martyr, with the blood of many Nobles and Worthies, and thousands of other Subjects: therefore the King of kings, in His gracious Providence, with his Vicegerent over these Kingdoms, hath placed your Lordship in the civil Watch-Tower of this Kingdom, to espy and prevent Sedition in the State, and consequently to have a watchful Eye against *Schism* in the Church; especially seing the great fundamental Maxim of some in this Kingdom, was not only dangerous to the State consequentially, and by its tendency, but substantially such.

And seing the purpose of this little Treatise is for healing and preventing of further *Schism* and *Error* in Judgment, tending to Sedition, I have presumed

The Epistle Dedicatory.

ed to intreat your Lordships Patrociny; for albeit it be little in quantity, yet its Subject-matter is so glorious, to wit, *Singing glory to our infinitely glorious God*; and the duty so unquestionable, that the Universal Church will joyn in the Practice with your Lordship, and say *Amen*; not only the reformed Churches, but also all these of the *Greek* and *Latine* Communion, yea, all Christians to the ends of the Earth.

My second Attractive, Are the many and rich Talents of Grace and Gifts with which the Father of Lights hath eminently endued your Lordship of knowledge and prudence, of Piety and Justice, of Zeal to the true Christian Religion, and Loyalty to his Majesty, by which your Lordships knowledge and deep Judgment, ye are able exactly to ponder the weight and validity of the Reasons brought to prove the lawfulness of singing the *Doxology*, and the levity and weakness of the pretended Reasons brought against it.

Therefore trusting your Lordship will follow his steps, on whom the Spirit of the Lord did rest, *the spirit of wisdom and understanding, the spirit of council and might, the spirit of knowledge and of the fear of the Lord*, Isa. 11. 2. And that you will piously observe the holy ways and stately steps of the Lord's Providence towards you, and so *understand the loving kindness of the Lord*, Psal. 107. Vers. last, and *Psal.* 111. 2. *The works of the Lord are great, sought out of all them that have pleasure*

there-

The Epistle Dedicatory.

therein; and the slighting of this pious and pleasant Duty, is a great sin, *Psal.* 28. 5. *Because they regard not the works of the Lord, nor the operation of his hands, he shall destroy them, and not build them up.* I am confident, your Lordship with much Spiritual-pleasure and joy in the Lord, hath observed his loving Kindness to you, as to another *Moses* drawn out of the Waters, *Exod.* 2. 10. to be a selected Servant, faithful in all the House of God, *Heb.* 3. 5. another *Eliakim*, on whose Shoulders the Lord hath laid the Government, *Isa.* 22. 20. and as your Lordships Father of blessed Memory died a Martyr for his Loyalty to his King, with many other Worthies; so our Kings Majesty, matchless for Piety in Life and Death, gave all these Worthies a meeting, in dying a glorious and royal Martyr for the Liberty of his loving Subjects; and as the wise and greatly beloved *Daniel*, one of the children of the *Babylonish* Captivity, of the seed of the Princes, was so endowed with gifts and graces by the Father of the Fatherless, that he was thought worthy to sit Judge in the gate of the Kingdom, *Dan.* 2. *verf.* last, So your Lordship, the son and heir of your Martyr Father, being a Fatherless-child of the late sad Captivity in *Scotland*, descending as the righteous heir from the ancient and honourable Family of the Barons of *Haddo*, one of the ancient Families in this Kingdom of *Scotland*, being cast upon the care of your heavenly Father, having enabled you by more then

ordinary

The Epistle Dedicatory.

ordinary gifts and graces, and advanced you through many orderly steps of Dignity, hath at last caused your Lordship to sit supream Judge in that very City and Judgment-seat, where your Father suffered so sad and unjust a Sentence; therefore shall Men say, *Verily there is a reward for the righteous, verily there is a God that judgeth in the earth,* Psal. 58. last verse.

The Fountain of Civil Honour is the Kings Majesty, and that Power and Priviledge he hath received from the King of kings, and accordingly, *Esther* 6.6. the word of the King was, *What shall be done to the man whom the King delighteth to honour?* but it is sure that the supream Fountain of this honour is the King of kings, who giveth forth a Rivolet of this Priviledge of Honour to all Kings under Him, so that when the King of kings, by His over-ruling and gracious Providence, puts it in the heart and hand of a Christian King under Him, to set his heart and eye upon a deserving and worthy Person; then the Glory of Gods stately steps of over-ruling Providence, and a work beseeming a gracious and a just King joyned together, is conspicuous and notour to every good Christian within that Sphere of Jurisdiction, and this same is the happy *juncto* of the King of kings, and his Vice-gerent in these united Lands for advancing your Lordship: What more suitable then this, for the son and heir of a royal Martyr Father, to advance the son and heir of a loyal Martyr Subject?

The Epistle Dedicatory.

Subject? As the Kings of kings is the Giver of every good Gift, so of Riches and Honour, and the Receiver is obliged to be thankful to the Giver, which thankfulness is best demonstrate in his improving these Talents to the glory of the Giver, to the good and comfort of his Neighbour, but the more comfortable advantage is that to his own Soul, a Spiritual gain of Peace with God, which passeth all understanding, and joy unspeakable and glorious, which is Heaven upon Earth, and conversing with better then Angels, having his conversation in Heaven, having the Heart mortified and crucified to the World, and all its Riches and Honours, which to them are loss and dross, being put in the ballance with Christ, *Phil.* 3. 7, 8. and as this is rare to be found to be honourable, and honoured of all Men, and yet to be humble, Riches to encrease, and yet not to set the Heart upon them, to abound in Plenty to the Cups running over, and yet be temperate, and the sensual and inferiour Powers of the Soul not to blind and then enslave the rational Powers thereof is rare to be found, and flows from more then ordinary Grace; hence your Lordship may well infer, that all the external Honour and Dignity which the Lord hath conferred upon you, which are good Gifts in themselves (and not to be slighted,) yet they are of far less value then the inward Spiritual and Heavenly Graces wherewith the God of all Grace hath beautified your Soul.

As

The Epistle Dedicatory.

As it is a matter of sad lamentation to the Godly, and of mourning in secret, when they see the evil example of great Ones so prevalent upon the lives of others, as Prophaneness to lift up the Horn, and Satan to erect his Throne, and Piety be Heart-broken, then slighted, then mocked, all which Sins kindle much Wrath, and bringeth down sore and inevitable Judgments upon a Land; so in the contrary, it is matter of great joy to all the Godly in the Land, for which they render hearty Praises to the God of Heaven, and looks upon it as a token for Good, (*that the Lord will make us glad, according to the days wherein he hath afflicted us, and the years wherein we have seen evil:*) even your Lordships good example, for the good example of the great, is more prevalent and effectual upon the Hearts and Lives of Men, then the most eloquent Oratry or convincing Reasons can prevail upon them, for the Orator is not able constantly to be beating upon the Ears of his Hearers, but will weary on his part, and the Hearers nauseat on their part; but for the good and holy example of the pious Life of the Great, is not an exhortation to Holiness once a Week, or once a Day, but continually without Interuption, and cries aloud without Noise, and insinuates without Affectation: Therefore, every pious Ruler, first, and most considereth the All-seeing-Eye of his Maker, to whom he must give account; so in the second place, he considereth the Eye of

his

The Epistle Dedicatory.

his Inferiour looking upon him, and ready to make the Rulers life and actions his Pattern, shining with all Grace and Vertue, will be so prevalent and conspicuous, that it will cause Prophaneness to be afraid and hide it self, and cause Piety and Vertue receive their due estimation and honour, that so the Lord's Glory and the Kingdom of Jesus may be advanced, and many Souls gained and saved, and thus the Lord may take pleasure in his People, and yet delight to do us good, and say, *Psal.* 132 *verf.* 14. *This is my rest, here will I dwell for ever, for I have desired it, and make our land* Hephziba *and* Beula; Which God of gods, and Judge of all the Earth, as He hath multiplied Honours upon your Lordship, so it is the Hope, Expectation, and Prayer of all good Subjects in this Land, that your Lordships chief study, and constant endeavour, may be, to promote the Lord's Glory, by a constant tenour of Piety and Justice, that *the mountains may bring peace to the people, and the little hills by righteousness,* Psal. 72. *verf.* 3. that ye may *raise up the foundations of many generations, and be called the repairer of the breaches,* Isa. 58. *verf.* 12.

That the Church and Kingdom may long enjoy your Lordship, as one of their great Blessings from the Lord; That Mercy and Truth may meet together, and Righteousness and Peace kiss each other, *Psal.* 85. So that by the good Hand of your God upon you, Truth and Piety, Order and Unity,

The Epistle Dedicatory.

Unity, Peace and Prosperity in Church and State may abound; that after many good days, ye may obtain that Approbation, *Well done good and faithfull servant, enter into the joy of thy Lord*; which is the sincere and fervent Prayer of,

Murrois, the 20. of
February, 1683.

Your Lordships most humble and devoted Servant,

ROBERT EDWARD.

ERRATA.

ERRATA.

IN the Preface, Page 4. Line 29. for *who*, read *which*. In the Contents, p. 2. l. 9. for *Cor.* r. *Chr.* p. 6. l. 42. for *Sam Satanius*, r *Samosatenus*. p. *ibid.* l. last, for *Serinium* r. *Syrmium*. p. 13. l. 8 for *videbent*, r. *viz.* p. 23. l 43. for *Roma*, r. *Tomo.* p. 41. l. 25 after αιδιω, add δοξη. p. 49. l. 18. for *university*, r. *universality* p. 45. l. 40. for λεγγε, r. λεγει. p. 65. l. 27. for *his*, r. *this*. p. 73 l. 30. for *care*, r. *cure*. p. 80. l. 30. for *Justinianum*, r. *Institutionum*. p. *ibid.* l. last, for *saved*, r. *received*. p. 89. l. 21. for *Desart*, r. *Desert*. p. *ibid.* l. 22. for *vers. 29.* r. *vers. 20.* p. *ibid.* l. 32. for *Sins* r. *for their Sin*. p. 91. l. 39. for *Isa. 4.* r. *Isa. 40.* p. *ibid.* l. last, for *word or reproach*, r. *words of reproach*. p. last, l. 11. for *Covenant*, r. *covenanted*. p. *ibid.* l. 17. dele *it*.

As for other literal Escapes, they are recommended to the discretion of the Christian Reader.

THE PREFACE
TO THE
CHRISTIAN READER.

HE *whose Name shall be called* Wonderful, Counseller, The Mighty God, The Everlasting Father, The Prince of Peace, *even He was truely called* Wonderful, *because of His two Natures, and there wonderful, if not also unspeakable union.*

(1) *Counseller, for in Him dwelleth all the treasures of wisdom and Knowledge,* Col. 2. 5. *The Mighty God, the same to us, a Child born,* Isa. 9. 6. *The Everlasting Father, and to us a Son given. The Prince of Peace being our Peace,* Eph. 2. 14, 15. *and Peace-maker, our Ransom and Redeemer, wonderful in His love to us, whose dimensions passeth Apostolick knowledge,* Eph. 3. 19. *who loved not His life unto the death, for his love was stronger then Death, who by His death was the death of Death,* Hos. 13. 14. *who hated His life being put in the ballance with His love to us. This wonderful Lover and Prince of Peace, died in bodily thirst, but His soul thirsting much more for our Salvation ; in His last Supper (which He left in Legacy to the Church His Spouse, as a love-Token,) Supper being ended, He inculcates Love and union as the badge of His Disciples,* John 13. 34, 35. *third and fourth time, and in His Prayer,*

(1) Ἐν δύο φύσεσιν ἀσυγχύτως, ἀτρέπτως, ἀδιαιρέτως, ἀχωρίστως, inconfuse, inconvertibiliter, indivulse & inseperabiliter, Concil. Chalcedon. Act. 5. Anno Domini 451. Episcop. 630. Quod & confirmatur in Synodo 6. Œcomen. Constantinop. Anno 681. Epis. 289. non modo quoad Christi duas naturas, sed & duas in eo voluntates naturales, & duas duarum naturarum & voluntatum operationes vel φυσικὰς ἐνεργείας ἀδιαιρέτως ἀτρέπτως ἀμερίστως ἀσυγχύτως, §. 8. & repetitum. §. 9. quoad operationes.

ἀρρήτως ὁ ἁπλοῦς Ἰησοῦς συνετέθη, ineffabiliter simplex Iesus compositus est Dionys. Areop. lib. de Div. nominibus, cap. 1. & Cyril. Alex. ἀρρήτως κ̀ ἀπεριηότως, ineffabiliter & incomprehensibiliter.

John 15. 12, 17. *the same again* John cap. 17. *after that His fare-*
well

The Preface to the Christian Reader.

well Sermon before His death, ingeminates His Petitions to His Father, that these whom thou hath given me, may be one, vers. 11. and 21. and the third time, vers. 23. Should not the Commands and Prayers of a dying Lord, and lover of His Brethren and Spouse, be highly regarded, and carefully obeyed, backed with the intreaties of the Holy Ghost by his Pen-man most pathetically. 1 Cor. 1. 10. *I beseech you brethren, by the Name of our Lord Jesus Christ, that ye all speak the same thing, that there be no divisions amongst you, that ye be perfectly joined together in the same mind, and in the same judgement,* Philip. 2. 2. *If there be any consolation in Christ, if any comfort in love, if any fellowship of the Spirit, if any bowels and mercies, fulfil ye my joy, that ye be like-minded, having the same love, being of one accord, of one mind*; So exceeding wonderfully the two Natures of God and Man were united, to unite Christians to God in Christ, and in them to one another, and our Saviour His body was rent to keep His Church from rent, His Soul and Body separate to keep His Church from separation; He prayed before His death for their union, He died to unite them, and the Holy Ghost, the God of Peace and Love, charges them in the Name of the Lord Jesus, to be united in one mind, and in one judgement; and yet alace, how many in this Land, who profess themselves the Brethren and Sisters of Jesus, left their first Love, and violated this commanded union with their Brethren and Mother Church of Scotland, *who did once hang upon her Breasts, and sucked the Breasts of her Consolations,* Isa. 66. 11. were dandled on her knees, and nursed with the *sincere milk of the word*, 1 Pet. 2. 2. yet too many of these, not only despise their Mother Church, but also run from her in scattered and confused Troups, as if they were fleeing in the day of Battel from the sword of the Pursuer, yea some cry out and swear they will lend their ear no more to their Mothers Instruction, they will have no more of her Milk, nor eat of her Bread in the Lords Supper, nor pollute their Children with her Baptism, and albeit their Mother cry after them with bowels of tenderest Christian compassion, they answer with disdain, *Stand by thy self, come not near to me, for I am holier then thou,* Isa. 65. 5. see what is the Lords answer to these, *these are a smoke in my nose, a fire that burneth all the day, and behold it is written, before me I will not keep silence, but will recompense, even recompense it into their bosome*; That your words to your Mother Church are the same in substance with these forecited in Isaiah, is clear to any impartial Reader, therefore I intreat you in the bowels of Jesus Christ, let not that fire and smoke of your Separation provoke the Lord any longer.

At present I intend not to survey all the particulars of the present Schism, but only this, viz. the refusing to sing the Doxology in the publick worship of God, which makes a sad and unchristian-like Rent, for in one Paroch-Church you may hear the Doxology Christianly sung, but in the next Paroch-Church no mention of it, nor in the wandring Conventicle at the Hill side, or in the Den, they have gone from Mountain to Hill, they have

forgotten

The Preface to the Christian Reader.

forgotten their resting place, *Jer.* 50.6. *and have forgotten the* Doxology, *as if they were all* Antitrinitarians, Jews, Turks, or Pagans, *yea, and too often in the same Church-Assembly, both in* City *and* Country, *when it comes to the closing of the* Psalm *some sing the* Doxology *decently, others sitting by who did sing the* Psalm *instantly turn silent at the* Doxology, *yea, some are worse, deriding and scoffing the* Singers *of it, this among* Christians *is a lamentation*, and shall be for a lamentation, *Ezek.* 19. 14. *tell it not in* Gath, *but (no doubt) it is proclaimed at* Rome *long ago, who rejoice in our halting, and say, aha, aha, our eye hath seen* : (2) *But lest the* Roman Church *insult against us, because some have separate from our* Church, *and thence infer that we are not of the true* Church, I answer, *that albeit a* Church *be* Orthodox, *some may depart from them, and no fault be in the* Church, *but in them that separate from her; dare any man impute a blot to the* Christian Church *in St.* John's *days, when there went some out from the* Apostolick Church, *when they were not of us, says the* Apostle, 1 Joh: 2. 19. *for if they had been of us, they had no doubt continued with us.* 2. *I answer,* These *who are separate from their* Mother Church, *and died in that time, I judge they have repented before the searcher of* Hearts, *and obtained* Mercy, *but the secret things belong to God, Deut.* 29. 29. *as for these of the* Separation *as yet alive, albeit they have fallen, they may arise, they have left their* Fathers House *with the* Prodigal, *but they may repent and return, for albeit they were bent on their* Separation, *as St.* Paul *on* Persecution *before his* Conversion, *so as he did it ignorantly, and therefore obtained* Mercy *upon his repentance*; 1 Tim. 1. 13: *so I judge in* Charity, *their* Seperation *flowed from their ignorance also, and therefore is a large door of* Hope *opened for* Mercy *to them upon their repen-*

(2) *Aquinas* in locum, 1 *Joh.* 2. 19. Erant de Ecclesia sacramentorum perceptione non charitatis communione, non erant ex nobis predestinatione aut electione, & ideo ex recessu eorum Ecclesia non est damnificata sicut nec corpus damnificatur cum humores pravi exeunt de corpore; nam si fuissent ex nobis prædestinatione aut electione mansissent utique nobiscum, *i. e.* finaliter mansissent in consolatione fidei, & idem summæ parte 1. quæst. 23. art. 4. in concl. omnes à deo prædestinati sunt electi & dilecti & art. 3. post concl. prædestinatio includit voluntatem conferendi gratiam & gloriam & resp. ad 2. Prædestinatio est causa gratiæ in hac vita, & gloriæ in vita futura imo, *Tridentini Sess.* 6. can. 15, & 16. Collatis fatentur prædestinatos ad vitam infallibiliter perseveraturos itaque Tridentini cum Aquinate sunt in hoc puncto Remonstrantibus multo Orthodoxiores, Lomb. itidem Sent. lib. 1. dist. 40. capitulo 1. Nullus prædestinatus potest damnari at labi & postmodum converti & salvari nam Schisma & Hæresis qua tales non sunt peccatum istud irremissibile at Ecclesia universalis penitenti absolutionem nequaquam negavit quum Deus misericors hanc

tance;

The Preface to the Christian Reader.

tance; *This answer will satisfie the most rational of the* Roman Church. 3. *I answer, Blessed be the God of order, who stilleth the noise of the Seas, the noise of their Waves, and the tumult of the People,* Psal. 65. 7. *who hath reduced the proud and swelling Waters of that deludge of Disorder, which threatned the overtopping of the Mountains, to abide within their wonted Channels; I wish these waters may abate more and more, and as with their Bodies they give external obedience to Order, so all this Church may be of one Heart and Soul, keeping the unity of the Spirit in the bond of Peace, it being observed, that the refusing to sing the* Doxology, *is the most known* Shibboleth, Judg. 12. 6. *whereby these of the Seperation are known from these that are orderly, and the refusing to sing it, proves a demonstration of too strong inclination to Separation; Therefore we resolve to take pains for its refutation, and if this opinion of the unlawfulness to sing the* Doxology *were meerly a speculative question in Divinity, and did not tend to practice, the knowledge thereof might safely and prudently be kept up from the Vulgar, for many such questions are wisely kept close within the walls of the Divinity School, which the Vulgar (although they did hear them dispute in their Mother Tongue) could not understand them: Not the less in these same questions the learned can dispute* pro *and* contra, *and be of contrary Judgements, and yet keep Love and Charity, but this Question anent the* Doxology *tends to Practice, and that in the publick worship of God, and that not only on the Christian Sabbath, but also on the Week day, and therefore the refusing to sing the* Doxology *is a daily stumbling to the weak.*

If any particular man, or particular meeting of Church-men, although they were a Body, Representative of many Particular Churches, yet it were Presumption in them, to press any Duty upon their Christian Brethren, who were not within their Line of Jurisdiction, but surely the Singing of the Doxologie, *is far otherwayes, for it hath the Authority, Approbation and Practise of the Universal Church, more then* 1300. *Years by past; which, (with the Lords assistance) we shall clear, from Antiquity, for in the* 2. *Greek Liturgies of* St. Basil, *and* St. Chrisostome, *who both lived in the* 4. Cent. *after our Lords Incarnation, The* Doxologie *is to be Seen, and Read unto this day; For these* 2. *Greek Liturgies, are used in the Publick Worship of God dayly, or weekly, sometime the one, sometime the other, in all the Churches of the Greek Communion, which contains thousand thousand Christians: In which Greek Liturgies,*

tabulam penitenti post naufragium concessit cui Doctrinæ S⁰. Claro adstipulatur, *Problem.* 30. *pag.* 255.

Δὸς ἡμῖν εν ενί σόματι και μία καρδία δοξάζειν και ανυμνεῖν τὸ παντιμον και μεγαλοπρεπὲς ὄνομα σȣ τȣ πατρὸς και τȣ υιε και τȣ πνεύματΘ ἁγιȣ νῦν και αεί και εἰς τȣς αιῶνας των αιώνων αμνὸ λαος, Chrisost. *Litur.* Pag. 20. gr. lat. Eandem Doxologiam habet *Basilius* in sua Lyturgia.

this

The Preface to the Christian Reader.

this Prayer is to be found in Greek, their Mother Tongue give unto us, That with one Mouth, and with one Heart we may Glorifie, and Sing Praise together, to the most Honourable and Magnificent Name of the Father, Son and Holy Ghost, now and ever, and to all Ages, Amen. The beginning, and foundation of which Prayer, is indyted by the Holy Ghost, Rom. 15. 6. That we may with one mind, and with one mouth glorifie God, even the Father of our Lord Jesus Christ. (a) *And according to this Prayer, from the rising of the sun, to the going down of the same, throughout the whole World,* where ever *Christianity is truly professed,* the Doxologie *is Sung, with one Heart, and with one Mouth unto this day;* except by *a few of late, in* Brittain; *whom I intreat seriously to consider these Questions, from that Text,* Rom. 15. 6. *Is it not God, Father, Son and Holy Ghost, who indyts that Prayer.* 2dly. *The hearing, and granting of that Prayer, throughout the Christian World, is it not the blessing of God, Father, Son, and Holy Ghost, in fulfilling the Christians Prayer, indyted by God Himself;* then dare any *Christian deny, that it is lawfull to sing Glory to God, Father, Son, and Holy Ghost, with one heart, and mouth: seing God, Father, Son, and Holy Ghost, commands and allowes Christians to glorifie Him, with one heart and mouth.*

(a) ἵνα ὁμοθυμαδὸν ἐν ἑνὶ στόματι δοξάζητε τὸν θεὸν καὶ πατέρα τοῦ κυρίου ἡμῶν Ἰησοῦ Χριστοῦ.

Upon consideration of the Blooding Wounds, and Torn Bowels of my Mother Church, in Christian compassion, I am pressed in Spirit, to speak a word in Her behalf, which I intend chiefly for two sort of Christians; First, *To these Babs in Christ, and of lesser knowledge, who are obedient to their Mother Church, and do not forsake this Her Law,* Prov. 6. 20. *of Christianity, but sing the Doxologie. Be ye stedfast and immoveable, be not drawn away from that Duty, by the evil Example, or Counsel of any, who would intise or mislead you, to increase their Soure Leaven, and Prosylits: I declare to you, as an Ambassadour of Christ, that you shal not have cause to repent you, of singing Glory to Father, Son and Holy Ghost, in the Day of your Account, to Father, Son and Holy Ghost; when the Grace of our Lord Jesus Christ, the Love of God, and the Communion of the Holy Ghost shall be with you, and your Grace consummat in Glory, and your Prayers turned into Hallelujahs: As for these who refuse to Sing the Doxologie, and think it a Sin to Sing it, or at least, have their doubts anent it, for want of better Information, these are of three Sorts.* 1. The weak Lambs, *who yet are seeking the way to Zion, and to please God in all good Conscience, to these I am willing to tender the sincere Milk of the Word, because of the Command of the Great Shepherd of our Souls,* John 21. 15. If you love me, feed my Lambs, *these I intreat in the bowels of Jesus Christ, to consider the danger of an Erronious Conscience; For St.* Paul was once, *yet more zealous then ye are, in a wrong way, of which*

The Preface to the Christian Reader.

he gave prudent and Christian warning to other Zealots, Acts 25.9. I verily thought with my self, that I ought to do many things contraire to the Name of Jesus of Nazareth, which thing I also did: *of which Erroneous Zealot Jews, he bears record,* Rom 10.2. That they have a zeal of God, but not according to knowledge; *So of you I judge in charity, that your Zeal is sincere, and abundant, but the defect is in your knowledge; and in such a case, the more Zeall, the more danger; and therefore be not Children in understanding,* 1 Cor. 14. 20. Be no more children tossed to and fro, and carried about with every wind of Doctrine, Eph. 4. 14. *Be aware to despise, or reject the Light of sound Instruction, and side no longer with* Antitrinitarians, *and the like Blasphemous Hereticks, all which the universall Church hath declared Excommunicat, as such, from the Communion of Saints, and forgivenness of Sins, side no more with these Monsters. The God of Truth reveall His Truth unto you, and give you understanding in all things; for to you I owe great compassion, and tendernesse of bowels: As for the* 2d. *Sort, called Christians, to wit, the cunningly painted Hypocrite, and the openly Prophane, I have a word alloted for them, reserved till near the close of the Treatise.*

Here I have an Apologie to make to the Learned, who may object, what needed so much to be written, to prove or defend that Practice, which none in the universal Church, for 1300. Years did call in question, to whom, in all humility I reply, these are not written for Information, or Reformation of the Learned, in this Point, who stand in need of neither, being assured, both of the Lawfulness, and Experiency of this Duty; but they also know, that there is too many of late years, in Scotland, who refuse to sing the Doxologie, to whom I am resolved to become all things to them all, whether weak, or more knowing, that by all means, I may gain some, for whose cause I have multiplyed Arguments to prove the lawfulnesse of the Doxologie, having to teach these weaned from the Milk, and drawn from the Breasts, to whom Precept must be upon Precept, and Lyne upon Lyne, Isa. 28. 9, 10. I hope none will say, that the Holy Ghost useth either Tautologie, or Battologie, in the foresaid 10: verse, when he doubles both the Precept and the Lyne; So I have brought, for Information of these little Ones, and Lambs of Christ; Reason upon Reason redoubled: For as the strong should have their stronger Food; So the Bab's their Milk: And some be more moved with one Reason, and some with another; herein I intending that great Pastorall Duty to do all things for Edrfying, 1 Cor. 14. 26. 2 Cor. 12. 19: And in Citing modern Divines, I have made most use of these, who will be most acceptable, and convincing to the Refusers of the Doxologie; And if at any time, (for defence of Truth,) I bring Proof from any bygone Practice of themselves, and their way, I here declare, that it no wayes to irritat, but to bear in the Truth with the more power, my purpose being to do all in Love, and what makes for Peace and Healing. *The Servant of the Lord must*

The Preface to the Christian Reader.

must not strive, but be gentle unto all Men, apt to Teach, patient, in meekneß Instructing those that oppose thimselves, 2 Tim. 2. 28. *and* 25.

That which is not written in the *Vulgar Tongue*, in this following little *Treatise*, in a *distinct Section* towards the *Right Hand*, is intended for the *Learned*.

Finally, I ingenuously declare, That my *first* and *chief End*, is the *Glory of God*, and I pray, through the *Lords blessing*, it may prove the *End*, and *Effect of the Work*: In the next place, I intend the *furtherance of the Peace*, and *Prosperity* of my *Mother-church*, in *Clearing*, and *Removing of mistakes*, among the *Children*, at *least*, to make the *Rent* and *Breach less*, that the *weak* might be *strengthened*, and *confirmed* in their *Judgement*, in their *Singing the* Doxologie, that the *Scruplous may be informed*, the *Averse convinced*, and *Reclaimed*, *Contentions* and *Swellings pacified*, and *removed*, as far as *Relates* to the *Doxologie*, that all with one Heart and Mouth may *Sing, Glory to God, Father, Son and Holy Ghost*, and *as my God and Saviour was subject to his Blessed* Virgin Mother, *and hath commanded me to be meek and lowly*, Matth. 11. 29. So in all due *humilitie*, as one of the *least* of the *Sons* of my *Mother Church*, what I have written on this Subject, in *submission*, I lay it down at her *Feet*, fully *resolving* to obey the *Law* of my *Father in Heaven*, which is not to *despise*, or *forsake* the *Law* of my *Spiritual Mother on Earth*. Prov. 1. 8. *and* Prov 6. 20. *That our Father in Heaven may have all the Glory, His Church Edification, and the Lambs of Christ their Milk, which shall be my desire, and Prayer at the Throne of Grace*.

THE

THE
CONTENTS
of the Several Chapters.

Chap. I.
Proveth the great Fundamentality of the Doctrine of the most blessed Trinity, from the Sacred Scriptures, and illustrateth it by Fathers, and Councils, and modern Divines; and answers the common Objection.

Chap. II.
Containeth a Catalogue of the chief Blasphemers of the Blessed Trinity, the first 400. Years, with the many evils of Sin and misery, that followed thereupon; and how the Lord from Heaven, and His Church on Earth, gave effectuall and prevalent Testimony against them.

Chap III.
Containeth the rise of the Arian Heresy, in the Fourth Century their Persecution, and Activity, their Falshood, Injustice, and Cruelty, and the Testimonie, both of God, and His Church against them.

Chap. IV.
The unanimous Practice, and Appointment of the universall Church, for Singing the Doxologie, be Occasion of Satan, and his Supposts great Opposition to the Doctrine of the Trinity, and in that their war against God.

Chap. V.
The cause of the continuance of the Doxologie, in after Ages, viz. The continuance of the Churches Persecution, and Temptation from Arians, and other Blasphemers of the Trinity, as Eutichians within, and Mahumitans without the Church; and the Rise and Growth of the Socinian Heresie, notwithstanding Gods witness against them, and the Church, and Magistrats endeavours in many Kingdoms, these Blasphemous Antitrinitarian Hereticks, remained and nesled with Anabaptists, and Quakers, all three Blasphemous Antitrinitarian Hereticks, which gives sufficient cause, for the continuance of the Doxologie.

Chap VI.
The lawfulness of Singing the Doxologie proven by these Arguments. 1: Because all Christians are Baptized in the Name of Father, Son, and Holy Ghost. 2. They believe, or profess their Faith, in Father, Son and Holy Ghost. 3. They believe Father, Son, and Holy Ghost to be their Creator, Redeemer and Sanctifier. 4. Their Faith, and Hope of Eternal Glory, is from Father, Son and Holy Ghost. 5: God, Father, Son and Holy

The Contents.

Holy Ghost made all things, and especially for His Glory. 6. This Lord of Glory often calls mans tongue His Glory. 7. From the practise of the Saints and Angels 8. From Gods Command 9. The Appointment and Practice of the universal Church. 10. The indivisibility of the worship we give to God one in Essence, and three Persons Illustrat by Fathers, and Councils.

Chap. VII.

The lawfulness of singing the Doxologie, proven by the induction of all it's Parts 12. from the three Holies Isa. 6. 3.

Chap. VIII.

13, Reason from that Song, Revel. 5. 9. 14. From Gods Command 1 Cor. 16. 20. Illustrat by Councils and Fathers.

Chap. IX.

15. Reason from the necessar Difference of the Christians worship, as in reading of the Word, Prayer, and Sacraments, they exceedingly differ from Christians, shal not then also be a difference betwixt the Christian singing of Psalms, and the Jewes, by singing the Doxologie. 16. As the Jewes in their Psalms of David, close many of them with a Doxologie, answering to the measure of their Light dispensed to them, in the Old Testament; So it becomes the Christian to have a Doxologie answerable to their greater measure of light of the Trinity in the New Testament. 17. Reason founded upon the signification of Jehovah Elohim, which is often in the Doxologie of the Old Testament.

Chap. X.

A Reason given for singing the Doxologie, satisfactory to every strong Christian, and that born in also upon the weak Christian, by Scripture Reason.

Chap. XI.

The Reasons why the General Assembly was not in power to lay aside the Doxologie, proving their great reluctancy to their own deed, with several other circumstances alleviating the same.

Chap. XII.

That invalid Scruple answered, because the Doxologie is not to be found altogether in one place of Scripture, and the conveniency of singing is proven.

Chap. XIII.

The many evils that flow from the refusing to sing the Doxologie.

Chap. XIV.

An exhortatory conclusion to the strong and orderly Christian, to receive and imbrace with all Christian Love, and tenderness every weak Christian, who shall return from their wandring in Error, to live in Order and unity in the Bosome of their Mother Church.

THE
DOXOLOGY
Approven.

CHAP. I.

The great fundamentality of the Doctrine of the most blessed Trinity, proven from the Sacred Scriptures, and illustrated by Fathers, Councils, and Modern Divines, and the great Objection answered.

Amongst all the Divine Mysteries of Christian Religion which it hath pleased God in His infinite Wisdom, Mercy & Goodness, to reveal to His Church on Earth, on which they are to build their Faith and Salvation, the Mystery of the Sacred Trinity one God in three Persons, is the first in order, and of great concernment; even the three that bear record in Heaven, the Father, the Word, and the Holy Ghost, and these three are one, 1 *Joh.* 5. 7. These three bear witness to the truth of all the Scriptures, then assuredly to this truth also, that they are three Persons in one Godhead, and among the twelve Articles of the Apostolick Creed, this Mystery of the Trinity takes up three.

In symbolo Athanasii ab ecclesia universali recepto, utpote in principio; & fine fidem in trinitate personarum esse necessariam ad salutem (ἵνα ἕνα Θεὸν ἐν Τριάδι καὶ Τριάδα ἐν μονάδι σεβώμεθα εἰ μή τις πιστῶς καὶ βεβαίως πιστεύσῃ σωθῆναι ε δυνήσεται) *bis asseritur.*

Zanchius de Deo, lib. 1. *part.* 1ᵃ *cap.* 1. §. 2. *quæstio de Trinitate, ut est omnium in Theologia creditu maxime necessaria, ita omnium cognitu difficillima.*

Meisnerus contra Socinianos scite probat plurimis argumentis, primum, & magnum articulum fidei christinæ esse unum Deum in Trinitate personarum quibus argumentis adstipulatur, Hoorn. Beek. *Socinianismi confutati.* 1. *lib.* 1. *cap.* 9. *à pag.* 226. *ad pag.* 243. *&* Voetius *select. disp. theol. par.* 1. *pag.* 472.

This sacred Mystery is most clearly manifested in our Saviour's Baptism, Mat. 3. 16, 17. Luk. 3. 21, 22. John 1. 32. 33. The Father speaks from Heaven, *this is my well-beloved Son*, while at the same time the Son is baptized in Jordan, and the Holy Ghost came down from Heaven in the likeness of a Dove, and lighted upon God the Son, and abode upon Him.

Moreover, The Sacrament of Baptism being ordained of God, Father, Son, and Holy Ghost, the first Sacrament of the Covenant of Grace ; in it all the Promises of Mercy and Salvation are sealed to Believers, and by it Christians are solemnly entered into the Church and House of God : so that the Contemner of this Sacrament debarreth himself from Salvation. Therefore God Himself hath appointed this Program to be prefixed upon the Porch of His Church, that this Almighty God In whose Name we are baptized, and in whom we Believe, is Father, Son, and Holy Ghost ; and it cannot be supposed, but that these Men and Women who were Proselyted, and being Pagans before, admitted to the benefite of Christian Baptism, behoved to take a time to learn the Grounds of their Religion : therefore the the Doctors of the Church, not only wrote Catechisms for these young Christians, who therefore, betwixt their first offering of themselves to the Christian Church, until the time they were baptized, were called *Catechumeni* ; These Doctors also wrote certain short

dogma de trinitate est fundamentale κατ'ἐξοχην ; imo fundamentum fundamenti, quia fundat alia dogmata fundamentalia ; quod multis ibid probat, & Melanct. loc. commun. cap. 27. summa Evangelii erudite comprehensa est in verbis baptismi.

Eusebius Pamphilus in conc. Niceno fatetur symbolum Nicenum paulis solum verbis differre à symbolo quod inquit nos ab episcopis antegressis accepimus, cumque lavatro baptismatis abluti essemus audivimus, Socrat. *hist. eccles. l.* 1. *c.* 5. *& Theodoret. lib.* 1. *cap.* 12.

Socrates *Hist. lib.* 7. *cap.* 17. *Judæus requirens baptizari, ante baptismi participationem multis diebus fidem christianam addiscere, cum precibus, & jejuniis præcipitur, idem cap.* 30. *lib.* 7. *gens Burgundorum à Paganismo conversa petit Baptismum quæ post septem dies in eis catechisandis impensos cum præce, & jejunio votum obtinuere hinc canon.* 46. Conc. Laodicen. *anno dom.* 364. *Baptizandos oportet fidei symbolum discere, & baptizanti reddere.*

Symbolum Con. Nicen. *anno. dom.* 325. Constantinopolitani *anno dom.* 381. Chalcedon. *anno dom.* 451. Symbolum Athanasii, *Symbolum quod habet* Irenæus *lib.* 1. *adversus Hæresis cap.* 2. *primum concilium* Toletan. conc. Lateranum *in omnibus prædictis symbolis habetur articulus trinitatis: & tanta cura Paganos Catechimenos articulum trinitatis docuerunt, ut* Lucianus *qui vixit sub* Trojano *anno dom.* 120. *formulam catechizandi catechimenos addisceret nam inducit Christianam sic sine*

Sums

Sums of Christian Faith commonly called Creeds, that before these Pagan Catechumein received Baptism, they were to give a confession of their Faith contained in their Creed; in all which Creeds, written by the Church, whether longer or shorter; and in their Catechisms, the Doctrine of the Trinity was a special part, and accordingly that Synod of Divines at *Westminster* in their lesser Catechism have not omitted the Trinity: So the reformed *French* Church in *Geneva* have a little Catechism, containing only twenty one short Questions, on which they examine these who are at first to be admitted to the Lords Table, which little Catechism begins with the Trinity, and is bound in with their *French* Version of the Bible, printed at *Geneva* 1567.

The Sacred Trinity being the Program of Christian Baptism, proved the strong and invincible Fort of the Christian Faith in the Trinity of Persons in the Godhead, against the *Arrians*, and other *Antitrinitarian* Hereticks: wherefore *Socinus*, who hath drunk much deeper in the poysonable Cup of Blasphemy against the blessed Trinity then the old *Arrians*, hath very slightingly written of the Sacrament of Baptism.

The second great Mystery of Christian Religion, is, that the Word was made Flesh, *Joh.* 1.14. and this the Holy Ghost calls the great Mystery of Godliness, God manifested in the Flesh, 1 *Timoth.* chap. 3. vers. 16. which Mystery, viz. that the Word, the second

Ethnicos catechizantem (licet animo blasphemo) Deum alte regnantem, magnum, ætherium, atque æternum filium patris, & spiritum sanctum ex patre procedentem unum ex tribus, & ex uno tria.

Patres Concilii Constantinopolitani *anno dom.* 383. *mittunt libellum Synodicam* Romam *ad Damasum, aliosque Episcopos ibidem convicatos, in quo exhibent fidei suæ Confessionem Fidei* Nicenæ *consentaneam και ακολυθον]α βαπ]ισμα]ι & consentaneam baptismati και διδασκεσαν ημάς πιςευειν εις]ο ονομα τε πα]ρος τε υιε και τε πνευματος αγιε, &* Nazianzenus *his contemporarius orat.* 32. *πιςευομεν εις πα]ερα και υιον και πνευμα αγιον ομοεσια τε και ομοδ'οξα εν οις και το βαπ]ισμα την]ελειωσιν εχει.*

Socinus *anno dom.* 1604. *scribit epistolam* Smaltio *itidem* Sociniano *de baptismo ut non necessario remittendo, atque ad synaxin excipiendis hominibus vitæ honestæ ac probatæ religionem christianam professis quamvis nunquam baptizatis: adeo abhorrent, ac si accipiendunt baptismum.*

Satan ut fidem nostram ab ipsis radicibus convelleret, partim de divina filii, & Spiritus Sancti essentia; partim de personali distinctione ingentes pugnas semper movebat, Calvin. *Institut. lib.* 1. *cap.* 13. §.21.

Servabat tamen Dominus in Papatu renascituri suo tempore populi semen, manebat salvus baptismus in Patris, Filii, & Spiritus Sancti nomen; quamvis peregrinæ linguæ usu, & multis aliis conspurcatus superstitionibus: manebat frustra toties oppugnatum unitatis essentiæ, & tri-

Person,

Person, God the Son was incarnate, and not the Father, or the Holy Ghost ; this cannot be known and believed aright, until first we know *nitatis personarum fundamentum, manebat doctrina de duabus Christi naturis,* Beza *epist.* 81.
& believe that there are three distinct Persons in the Godhead, therefore our Saviour, *Joh.* 17. 3. joyns these two together, *This is life everlasting, to know thee the only true God, and Jesus Christ whom thou hast sent*; and the Apostle *Paul*, Coloss. 2. 2. *to the acknowledgment of the mystery of God, and of the Father, and of Christ.*

If it be objected, that it seems to be a hard saying, That the Knowledge and Faith in God, and three Persons, Father, Son, and Holy Ghost, and in Christ God and Man in one Person, is necessary to Salvation : Seing both these are profound Mysteries, so far above Humane Reason and Capacity, I answer, first, Not only these two are great Mysteries, but also the whole Gospel is a Divine Revelation of a continued tract of Mysteries, *Mark* 4. 11. *Rom.* 16. 25, 26. *Eph.* 3. 9, 16, 19. *Coloss.* 1. 26, 27. called the great Mystery of Godliness, 1 *Tim.* 3. 16. for there is no other Name under Heaven given among Men, whereby we must be saved, but the Name of Jesus, *Acts* 4. 12. who is the Captain of our Salvation, *Heb.* 2. 10. the Author of Eternal Salvation, *Heb.* 5. 9. and the Gospel is called the Knowledge of Salvation, *Luk.* 1. 77. the Word of Salvation, *Acts* 13. 26. the Way of Salvation, *Acts* 16. 17. the Salvation of God, *Acts* 28. 28. the Power of God to Salvation, *Rom.* 1. 16. the great Salvation, *Heb.* 2. 3. so that whosoever will not believe these Gospel Mysteries, is damned. I answer secondly, that to Divine and Saving Faith, as such demonstrative knowledge in the Logical Sense, far less comprehensive knowledge is required ; but the Lord condescending to Mans Humane weak Capacity, accepts of Faith, albeit apprehensive Knowledge go before it, not alwayes requiring that they know how such a thing is true, but that howsoever it is true : And because of the mysteriousness of these Gospel Divine Truths, there is a necessity for a Christian to deny himself, before he can follow Christ, *Matt.* 16. 24. deny his carnal Wit and corrupt Reason, therefore in the Lord's work of Man's Conversion, in which He applys His exceeding great and Mighty Power, *Eph.* 1. 19. He casts down Imaginations, and every high thing that exalteth it self against the Knowledge of God, and bringeth into captivity every thought unto the obedience of Christ, 2 *Cor.* 10. 5. where albeit the Almighty Hand of God is first in order, and chief in the work, yet the Christian himself, willingly consents to captivate all his carnal Imaginations and Thoughts, and over the belly of them all, gives the assent of Faith to the Mysteries of the Gospel, because they are the Truth of God, who is infinite in Truth, and cannot Lie ; for he who piously and humbly captivates his Thoughts to Christ, will stop the mouth of all Objections of corrupt Reason, with *Abraham, against*

against hope believing in hope, Rom. 4. 18. which assent of Faith gives God far more Glory, then the assent of Science, which flows naturally from the force of that natural Light, born in by the knowledge of the Cause; but the assent of Faith is supernatural, being a supernatural Grace and gift of God, with all its degrees: And because the Mystery of the Trinity, and Christ's Incarnation, were so high above Man's corrupt Reason, therefore in the first 400. Years of the New Testament, Satan wrought mightily in the Children of Disobedience, and did find it an easie work to raise up many blasphemous Hereticks, who in the pride of their undaunted Heart, refused to captivate their corrupt Reason to believe the Mysteries of the Trinity and Incarnation, which were not contrary to Reason, but above it.

CHAP. II.

This Chapter hath three Parts First, *a Catalogue of the Chief Ringleading Hereticks, against the Doctrine of the Sacred Trinity, the first 400. Years.* Secondly, *The many evils of Sin and Misery, that followed upon these Heresies.* Thirdly, *How the Lord and His Church opposed and confounded them.*

AS for the Roll of the Ring leading Hereticks, after our Lord's Ascension, (intending brevity) We passe by all the Errors, or Heresies mentioned or foretold in the New Testament. *Matth.*24. *v* 9. and 24. *Act.* 20. *v.* 29, and 30. *Acts* 15. *Rom.* 16. *v.* 17, and 18. *Gal.* 1. 6, 7. *Col.* 3. *v.* 1. *Col.* 9. *v.* 10. *Col.* 2. *v.* 8. 1 *Tim.* 1. 20. *Col.* 9. 1. 2 *Tim.* 2. *v.* 17, 18. 2 *Tim.* 3. 8. 2 *Thess.* 2. *v.* 8. Albeit therein be instanced diverse Doctrines of Devils, and St. *Peter* foretells, *that some would deny the Lord that bought them*, 2 *Pet. v.* 4. and St. *John* 2 *Epist.* 4. 3. mentions many Antichrists in the General, and denyers of Christ, but particularizeth none as such; for *Simon Magus*, Act. 8. 18. Was a baptised Christian, and falling in the Sin of *Simonie* in a most grosse manner, was justly and bitterly rebuked by the Apostle *Peter*: And Ecclesiastick Hystoriographers record, that thereafter he returned with the Doge to his vomite, and with the Sow, to the wallowing in the myre; went to *Rome*, and turned to his old trade of witchcraft, where he was admired for his Lying Satanical Wonders (as before his Baptism) he had been admired in *Samaria, Act.* 8. *v.* 9, 10. and blasphemously called himself, Father, Son, and Holy Ghost. (b) *Cerinthus* blasphemed Christ Jesus to be only a Man, and not the *Messia*. *Anno Dom.* 75.

(b) *Euseb. hist. Eccles. lib.* 2 *cap.* 1. *& cap.* 12. 13, 14. *Ignatius Epistola ad Tralesios Irenæus, lib.* I. *cap.* 20. *Justinus Martyr, Apologia secunda Justus.*

The

(c) The third Ring-leader Heretick *Ebion*, vented the like Blasphemies; by occasion of which three Hereticks, and their many followers, the Apostle St. *John*, who lived to this time, wrot the Gospel, in which his chief intent is to prove, and maintain against these Blasphemous Hereticks, that Christ is God and Man in one Person. (*d*) *Cerdon* Blasphemed, that the God of the Old Testament was not Christ's Father, *Anno Dom.* 143. (*e*) *Valentinus*, of whom came the *Genosticks*, rejected the Doctrine of the Sacred Trinity, and made up a fiction as it were of three Gods, *Anno Dom.* 145. (*f*)

(*a*) *Theodotus*, That Christ was only Man, he denyed Christ to be the Word *Joh.* 1. 1. *An. Dom.* 194.

(*b*) *Praxeas* denyed the Trinity, his followers were called *Patripossiani*, *Anno Dom.* 210.

(*c*) *Melchizedeciani* blasphemed, that *Melchizedeck* was greater then Christ.

(*d*) *Sabellius* denyed the blessed Trinity.

(*e*) *Samosatenus*, denyed Christ to be God, *Anno Dom.* 269.

(*f*) *Manes* and his Followers denyed Christ, and the Holy Ghost to be God.

(*g*) *Arius*, denyed the second Person of the blessed Trinity to be one in substance, co-equall and co-eternall with God the Father, he was confuted in the Council of *Nice*, his Blasphemy condemned, and he Excommunicated, *An. Dom.* 325.

(*h*) *Photinius* fell unto the heresie of *Sabellius* and *Sam. Satanius*, he was condemned in the Council of *Sirinium*.

(*c*) *Irenæus*, *lib.* 1. *cap.* 15. & *lib.* 3. *cap.* 3. *Euseb. lib.* 3. *cap.* 22.

(*d*) *Irenæus lib.* 1. *cap.* 26. *Eusebius lib.* 3. *cap.* 21. *Ignatious epist. ad Trallianos*, *Epiphanius heresie* 51.

(*e*) *Irenæus lib.* 1. *cap.* 28. *Euseb. lib.* 4. *cap.* 10.

(*f*) *Euseb. lib.* 4. *cap.* 10. *Irenæus lib.* 1. *cap.* 1. & *alibi passim multis refutat.*

(*a*) *Euseb. lib.* 5. *cap. ult.* Eum cum prioribus refutat, Ignatius, nominatim *Epist. ad* Trallianos.

(*b*) *Hos refutat* Tertul.

(*c*) *Hos refutat.* Tertul.

(*d*) *Eus. lib.* 7. *cap.* 5. *refutatur ad* Athanasio.

(*e*) *Damnatus in Concilio Antiocheno, Anno Dom.* 272.

(*f*) *Eus. lib.* 7. *c.* 25. *Socrat.* 1. *lib.* 1. *cap.* 17. *Exortus est* Anno Dom. 276. *cum* Augustinius *multus & eruditus refutavit.*

(*g*) *Damnatus a* 318. *Episcopis,* Socret. *lib.* 1. *cap.* 3, 4. 5. Theodoret. *lib. cap.* 1. 7. Sozomen *lib.* 1. *cap.* 16. Anno Dom. 325.

(*h*) Socrat: *lib.* 2. *cap.* 24. *a* Basilio *magno in disputatione devictus.*

The Doxology Approven. 7

(*i*) *Macedonius*, denyed the Holy Ghost to be God, *Anno Dom.* 360. He was condemned in the General Council of *Constantinople*, *Anno Dom.* 381.

(*k*) *Nestorius*, denyed the Personal Union of Christ's Divine and Humane Natures, Therefore was condemned by a General Council at *Ephesus* by 200. Bishops, *Anno Dom.* 431. And being obstinat, was banished by the *Emp. Theodosius.*

(1) *Socrates, lib. 2. cap.* 35. *ab* Athanasio *&* Basillo *refutatus.*

(*k*) Socrat. *lib. 7. cap. 33. in hoc concilio contra* Nestorium Cyrillus *magnam sustinuit partem.*

Albeit these forementioned Hereticks all Blasphemed the Sacred Trinity, yet none of them, but were poysoned with moe Errors besides, for mans corrupt heart is a too fertill soil to receive Satans Inventions.

(*l*) One of the Antients, by reading the Blasphemies of Hereticks, did not only condemne them, but also abhorred them the more; So I wish every Christian Reader of this Little Catalogue to

(1) Dionisius *Episcopus* Alexandrinus. Eus. *lib. 7. cap. 6. Anno Dom.* 250.

make the like good use of it, for the Learned read them at length, in the large Volums, and from this Catalogue, the Learned may Collect the Reason, why the subtill Serpent, the Enemy of Gods Glory, and Mans Salvation, was so much set against the Doctrine of the Trinity; even because of it's great fundamentality, in the Christian Saving Faith.

In the second Part of the Chapter follows the manyfold, and sade evils, both of Sin and Misery that were caused by these Blasphemous Hereticks.

1. The Lord of Glory was in a High Degree dishonoured, and greatly provoked to anger; So that the Learned, and Pious, in there consuming Zeal, and holy Indignation, did admire the Lords long Suffering Patience; crying out, *O God how long shal the adversary reproach? shall the enemy blaspheme thy name for ever?* Psal. 74. 10.

2. Too many followed those Blaspheming Hereticks, and their Pernitious wayes, and that often in the particular Kingdom, where their Blasphemy was first invented, and sometimes their Pestilentious Breath spread abroad, and infected moe Kingdoms with their Poyson.

3. Satan, and the power of Darknesse sometimes seemed to triumph, and Wickedness to lift up it's horn on high, and the smoak of the Bottomless Pit to darken the Face of the Earth.

4. Many weak Christians, and tender Limbs of Christ staggered, and stumbled, being troubled with the Words of Hereticks, almost to

the subverting of their Souls, now in a fainting condition, their hearts, being moved as the Trees of the Wood with a mighty Wind? and many in danger to perish, for whom Christ died.

5. The sade condition of these Flocks, no doubt, moved their Pastors, in holy Zeal, like St. *Paul*, to wish these Incorrigible Hereticks, who did what in them lay, to destroy the Flock of God, A curfed from the Lord, as they were cut off from the Church, *Gal.* 5. 12. even these wandring Stars, to whom is reserved the blackness of darkness for ever, *Jude v.* 13.

6. So netime unstable Church-men, were Deceived, and Insnared, who, when Learned, Eloquent, or both, they prevailed mightily, both in City and Countrey; Like that time, when the Great Red Dragons Tail, did draw the third part of the Stars of Heaven, and cast them to the Earth, *Revel.* 12. 3 4. Hence a fearfull Rent, and Schisme was made in the Church; Hence came Biting, Devouring, and Consuming one another, *Gal.* 5. 15.

7. The *Jew* and *Pagan*, were hardened in their Errors, and a stumbling block insuperable laid in the way of their Conversion.

8. The *Jew*, (and in after Ages the *Turk* joyning with them) did gladly grasp at the opportunity, to increase the Fire of Contention, by joyning with the Hereticks and Apostats, and strengthning their hands against the Orthodox; And took the more boldnesse to Blaspheme that worthy Name by which we are named, *Iam.* 2. 7.

9. The frequent and beautiful meetings of the Flocks of Christ, being Seduced, Diminished, and *Scattered*, caused their Faithful Pastors to offend, Mourn and Lament these of their Flocks that had fallen; Like the Loving Mother, weeping over, not One only, but Many of Her Children dying together: And to ly all night in Sackcloath, and weep betwixt the Porch and the Altar, to be in great heaviness, and continual forrow of heart, and almost to wish themselves accurfed from Christ, for the welfare of His Church, and their Flocks therein, *Rom.* 9. 21.

10. When sometime the Faction of Hereticks grew strong, as in particular of the *Arians*, having, by the subtility of the Serpent, obtained the Secular Power to joyn, and side with them, and so did many Years Persecute the true Church of Christ, not only to the spoyling of their Goods Imprisonment, or Banishment, but also many thousands having suffered Cruel Torments, at last Sealled the True Faith of Christ with their Blood and Death: Of which *Arian* Persecution against the true Church of Christ, we intend hereafter to give you a more particular accompt.

Follows the third part of the Chapter, wherein we shall give you a Compendious accompt of the Good and Holy Means which the God of Truth, who walks in the midst of the seven Golden Candlesticks,

and

The Doxology Approven.

and His Church the Pillar, and Ground of Truth, 1 *Tim.* 3. 15. Having the Truth dwelling in them, and therefore were Fellow-helpers to the truth: In this time of *Jacobs* trouble; Winnowing, and Fiery Tryal; The Lord stirred up, and inspired the Learned Doctors of His Church, to plead the cause of their Mother, against these Wolves and Foxes, who made Havock of the Church: which Doctors, in their Generation were Burning and Shining Lights, did earnestly contend for the Faith once delivered unto the Saints, *Jude* 3. Were valiant for the Truth, and suffered it not to fall in the Streets; but gave those Hereticks publick Dispur, as they found Opportunity; Refuted them by their Writings, left to the Church in their several Volums to this Day, wherein they Refuted not only the Heresies that rose in their own Dayes, but also all the Heresies that Blasphemers had spread before their time, and by Painfull and Zealous Preaching of the Truth, they Confirmed their Flocks, and furnished them with Powerfull preservatives against the Poyson of Seducers.

(*2*) A second Mean, Beside the thousand thousand Christians that Sealed the Christian Faith of the Trinity with their Blood, and Death; among them many Pious, and Learned Bishops, not only defended the Truth of God by their Pen, and Writings, as aforesaid; but also Sealed that Truth which they had Written, and Preached, by their Blood and Death; As *Ignatius*, *Justin*, *Irenæus* and *Cyprian*, and many others, who wrot learnedly in defence of the Sacred Trinity, against Blasphemous Hereticks.

The third Means, As these glorious Martyrs, for the Glory of their Lord, Father, Son and Holy Ghost, Sealed His Truth with their Blood: So the Almighty, who only does wonders, appended His own Seall to His own Truth, in their Death, by many miracles of diverse sorts. *First*, of stupendious Courage, and (*2*) Joy given them from above, to the Admiration and Confusion of their

(1) *Ignatius* & *Justinus in suis Epistolis* Justinus *epistola ad Philippenses Dominus mittens Apostolos jussit baptizare in nomen Patris Filij & Spiritus Sancti* ὅ ἐς εἰς ἕνα ἰδιώνυμον, ὅ τε εἰς Ἰησοῦς ἐνανθρωπήσαντας, ἀλλὰ εἰς Ἰησοῦς ὁμοίως, & *Epist. ad. &c. Philadelphienses.* εἰς ἀγένητος ὁ θεὸς καὶ πατὴρ καὶ εἷς μονογενὴς υἱὸς θεὸς λόγος καὶ ἀνθρωπος καὶ εἰς παράκλητος τὸ πνεῦμα τῆς ἀληθείας. *quod ad Ignatium in suis multis epistolis ad varias Ecclesias perquam erudite omnes Hæreticos se priores confutat, confundit præsertim antitrinitarios* (3.) *Irenæus justo volumine & summo labore scripsit polemice adversus Hereticos se priores & contemporarios.* (4) *Cyprianus justo itidem volumine multus est in veritate christiana stabilienda quam hi quatuor heroes sanguine consignarunt.*

(2) *Ignatius, a militibus Romam conductus in Epist. quam ad Romanos præmisit, vehementer christianos hortatur, Romanos & adjurat*

D 2 their

their tormenting Enemies. 2*dly*: Miracles manifested without them in their Death, as the Learned may read in the Church History; often the wild beasts refusing to devour them, and sometimes the fire to burn them. (*b*) Yea; 3*dly*. the Lord wrought many Glorious Miracles at the Graves of Martyres after their Death, of which there are many Examples in the Church History.

The *Fourth Mean*, whereas *Solomon* faith, *in the multitude of counsellers there is safety*; Therefore the Doctors of the Primitive Church did meet in Councils, as they saw need, in this or that Kingdom; but sometimes also, they did meet more solemnly in greater numbers. sometimes 3, or 4. sometimes 600 Bishops together, besides moe then the double number of Presbyters, and these of the most Learned, and Pious Divines, that were in the Christian World, out of *Asia*, *Affrica*, and *Europe* by long, and perilous journies, crossing Sea, and Land, beginning with (*a*) fasting and praying. To which Councils *respective*, the then reigning Hereticks were Summoned to appear, and appearing were examined anent their Errors, their Errors refuted and sometime, yet seldome, themselves converted, but if obstinat, their mouths stopped; their Errors, and Blasphemies condemned, and accursed; themselves Excommunicat; and sometimes also Banished by the supream civil Magistrate, and for the furder confirmation of the Faith of following Generations, and establishment of the Posterity in the Truth. The Church did put in register, the proceedings of these famous Councills, whether Nationall, or Generall against these severall Hereticks: As also their severall Acts, for Order and Decency, which Books are extant to this day in great Volumes.

As for these Hereticks, albeit the Lord did permit them for a season, to try His People, if they would cleave to His Truth, or not, *Deut*. 13. 3. And that the approved might be made manifest, 1 *Cor*. 11. 13.

ut eorum nullus folicitet magistratum Romanum ut Ignatium a morte liberate; fassus se exultaturum tormenta, & mortem pro Christo subire; & martyrium evadere se omnino abnuere; sed inflexibiliter desiderare: qualis fortitudo in pluribus martyribus fuit conspicua.

(*b*) *Hujus instantia in Polycarpi martyrô commemorantur hæc miracula in itinere ad ignem voce è Cœlo confortatur 2.dum stat in igne ingens flamma ad distantiam corpus circumvallat, quasi sanctum dei attingere renuens ita ut miles illud observans* [*flamma crudelior*] *Policarpi corpus bastâ confoderit* (3) *sancti combusti corpus suavissimum, & fragrantissimum emisit odorem Euseb. hist. Eccles. lib. 4. cap. 14.*

(*a*) *Patres Synodi Nicerni jejunium indixerunt.ut Deus utilitati Ecclesiarum consultum vellet*, Teodoret *in ancorato*.

The Doxology Approven.

11: 13: Yet the Lord blessed the pains of His faithfull Servants against them, So that these Storms were turned to a Calme, and these Hereticks wholly made known, and He who sets bounds to the proud waves of the Sea, set also bounds to Satans Malice; and put a hook in the nose of these Blasphemers.

The *Fifth* Mean, The Lord from Heaven did manifest His Wrath and Indignation signally against some of the speciall Ring-leading Hereticks, or else by the hand of the civil Magistrat.

(b) *Simon Magus*, at *Rome*, by the help of Devils did flee in the Air; but fell down and was bruised to death, at the prayers of the Apostle *Peter*.

Secondly, Elimas the Sorcerer, was by God, miraculously smitten with blindness, for his Anti christian perverseness, *Acts* 13. 11.

(c) *Thirdly, Montanus*, and his Prophetess *Maximilla* hanged themselves.

(d) *Fourthly, Theodotus* by force took his flight towards Heaven, but fell down, and died miserably.

Fifthly, *Buddas* or *Terebinthus*, *Nicen* through Sorcery did flie up in the Air, but fell down and brake his neck.

(e) *Sixthly, Manues* a *Persian* Heretick, the King of *Persia* caused take off his skin, flayed alive, filled it with Chaffe, and hanged it up at the Gate of the City.

(a) *Seventhly, Arius* being observed by the Bishop of *Alexandria*, that he was a dangerous

(b) Eus. *lib.* 2. *cap.* 1. 13, 14. Egesippus *lib.* 3. *cap.* 2. Epiphanius *lib.* 2. *her.* 22.

(c) Eus. *lib.* 5. *cap.* 15, 18.

(d) Eus. *lib.* 5. *cap.* 14.

(e) Socrat. *lib.* 1: *cap.* 17.

(f) Socratas *lib.* 1: *cap.* 21.

Heretick and mighty proud, while he is under Process, intends to come to the Church of *Alexandria* to morrow, in a presumptuous manner? wherefore the Bishop, all that night stayed in the Church, with Fasting, and Prayers and Tears wrestling against *Arius*; who, to morrow going to that Church, a sudden Terror of Conscience, and vehement looseness of Belly did assault him, that he was forced to go aside to the next publick Jacks, where all his bowells gushed out; a fit
Death.

Death-bed for so vile an excrement of Satan, whose breath had bred the most deadly pestilency that ever was in the World, whose manner of Death was a mercy to the World, and a Beaken of his Shipwrack, fixed by the Almighty, upon the dangerous Rock of his Blasphemous Heresie.

(*g*) Eightly, *Priscbillianus*, (g) *Prosper in chronico.* *Anno Dom*:400. being, condemned by a Church Council at *Burdeaux* for his Blasphemies against the Trinity, with others of his Stamp, was beheaded by the Emperour *Maximus*. All the foresaid Blasphemers of the Trinity, the Lord stigmatized with a miserable death, to the terror of others.

CHAP. III.

Containeth the rise of the Arian Heresie *in the Fourth Century, their Persecution and Activity, their Falshood, Injustice and Cruelty; and the prevalent Testimony both of God and His Church against them.*

AS In the first 300. Years after our Lord's Ascension, His Church was sore vexed by Ten bloody Persecutions, raised by *Pagan* Emperours, and molested by *Antitrinitarian* Hereticks, of which we have given you a short view in the former Chapter; So in this fourth Century, Satan the Father of Lies, *Anno Dom.* 324. filled the Heart of *Arius* (a proud Presbyter in *Alexandria*) with Blasphemies against the second Person of the Blessed Trinity; wherefore, the famous Council of *Nice*, consisting of 318. Bishops, conveened partly for examining and confounding of *Arius* Error in the Year 325. where after long dispute granted to the Adversary, his blasphemous Error was condemned, and he Excommunicate: Notwithstanding, thereafter his Errors spread like a Gangren, and that chiefly by occasion of two Emperours *Constantius* and *Valence*, whom the *Arians* seduced to their Heresie, and so the *Arian* obtaining the Arm, and Countenance of the Civil Power to their wicked Faction, they left no mean unessyed to encrease and strengthen their Party, and spread their Poison, which we intend to treat of in this Chapter, in these particulars.

First, Their indefatigable pains in conveening Church Councils. *Secondly*, The Falshood and Injustice in their Proceedings. *Thirdly*, Their hellish Policies. *Fourthly*, Their monstruous Cruelty against the Orthodox. *Fifthly*, The Lord's witnessing against them, both by His Church and His own immediate Hand of Justice upon them. To return to the first of these, in imitation of the Orthodox and true Church, like Satan, they transformed themselves into Angels of Light, did conveen Councils, sometime in one City and Kingdom, and sometime

time in another, as they judged most expedient for their purpose; where they composed diverse Creeds, but all Heterodox, and differing from the *Nicen* Creed; * Their first Council held at *Tyrus*, (*a*) The second at *Jerusalem*, The third at *Antioch*, where they composed their first *Arian* Creed, (*b*) Fourthly, Four prime leading *Arians* presented to the Emperour a second *Arian* Creed, (*c*) Fifthly, The *Arians* in the East sent a long Creed to the Bishops in the West, which they rejected. (*d*) Sixthly, At *Syrmium* in *Illyria* the *Arians* wrote two Creeds, (*e*) Seventhly, In a Council at *Ariminum*, the *Arians* wrote a sixth Creed, (*f*) Eightly, At *Nica* in *Thrasia* the *Arians* wrote a Creed, which deceitfully they called the *Nicen* Creed, (*g*) Ninthly, The *Arians* held a Council at *Seleucia* in *Isauria*, (*h*) Their last two Councils they held at *Constantinople* and *Antioch*, where they Decree, that the word Substance (*i*) and Person, of one Substance, of another Substance, all these (*k*) be expunged out of all Creeds; By all which we may perceive the *Arian* applying all his Oars, going to and fro, and walking up and down in the Earth, compassing Sea and Land to conveen Councils, thereby to frame Mischief by a Law, to engage and inslave unstable Souls, by the Shadow of a Chruch Sanction, making Proselytes, strengthening his Faction.

* Socrat. *lib.* 2. *cap.* 32. *In fine breviter colligit numerum symbolorum Arrianorum particulatim & oppidatim novem videbent.*
(*a*) Socrat. *lib.* 1. *cap.* 22.
(*b*) Socrat. *lib.* 2. *cap.* 14.
(*c*) Socrat. *lib.* 2. *cap.* 14.
(*d*) Socrat. *lib.* 2. *cap.* 14.
(*e*) Sozomen *lib.*3. *cap.*10. Socrat. *lib.*2. *cap.*25.
(*f*) Socrat. *lib.*2. *cap.*29. Sozomen *lib.*4. *cap.*16.
(*g*) Sozomen *lib.*4. *cap.*18.
(*h*) Socrat. *lib.*2. *cap.*32.
(*i*) Theodoret. *lib.*2. *cap.*31.
(*k*) Ariani *multis pseudosynodis convocatis in quatuor factiones abiere, quarum quæque priore insanior, prima factio petit in omnibus symbolis hoc expungendum quod filius sit patri* ὁμοούσιος: *factio secunda quod sit in symbolis exprimendum filium esse patri* ὁμοιούσιον, *tertia factio filium esse patri tantummodo* ὁμοιον: *quarta factio filium esse patri* ἀνομοιον *dissimilem & hi sunt appellati anomœi, &* ετερουσιοι *&* εξουκουντες, *quod blasphemarent filium esse* ἐξ οὐκ ὄντων *ex non existentibus hi expreße damnantur in symbolo Niceno & hujus quartæ factionis fuit ipse* Arius Sozomen *lib.*4. *cap.*21,28.

Having spoken of their indefatigable Pains, let us in the *second* place observe their deceitful Dealling, their Deeps and Devices, which the Father of. Lies (the old and crooked Serpent) had taught them: First, *Eusebius* Bishop of *Nicomedia* being justly degraded by that Orthodox Council of *Nice*, for his obstinacy in *Arianism*, and he, together

ther with *Arius*, banished by the Emperour *Constantine*, he wrote to the Emperour a penitential Letter, wherein he subscrived the *Nicen* Creed, (*a*) (but with a double Heart,) and so was restored to his Place and Function; and *Arius* followed his example, (*b*) both in subscriving and dissembling, remaining in the gall of Bitterness with *Simon Magus*, and in the Synagogue of Satan; wherefore shortly thereafter the Lord purged His Church of *Arius*, by an extraordinary and horrible death, even then when he was in the height of his Pride, going to that Church in grandour, where he had spewed out his Blasphemies against the Son of God, even that King of Saints, who thought it no robbery to be equal with His Father, commands him to halt, not permitting him to enter into the House of God to pollute it, but thrust him into a common Jacks by the way, where the Lord cast out all his Intrals with his Excrements, and cast him effectually out of His Church, and stopped his blasphemous Mouth. Notwithstanding all this great and visible Judgment on *Arius*, his Brother in Evil (*Eusebius* of *Nicomedia*) would not learn Righteousness, but hardened his heart in Pride, turned an obstinate and violent Persecuter of the true Church and Saints, (*c*) and chief Leader of the *Arian* Faction, adding Perjury to his Blasphemy.

(*a*) Socrat. *lib.*1. *cap.*10.
(*b*) Socrat. *lib.*1. *cap.*19.

(*c*) Socrat. *lib.*1. *cap.*25.

Thirdly, As the *Arians* were Perfidious in their beginning, so in their Progress, they learned at the Accuser of the Brethren, to turn impudent false Accusers of the Orthodox Church men, which they acted in these forementioned pretended Church Counsels; And first, the great *Athanasius*, who as a divine Hero, stood in the Breach for the true Church, to whom both the *Emperour* and Bishop of *Rome* deferred great respect in their Letters, (*d*) yet him they strived to affront in their Councils, and falsly accuse that he had cutted off a Man's Hand, which Hand they produced in their Council, having the Man himself fast in Prison; but by good and remarkable Providence, the Man escaped out of their Prison, and came to *Athanasius* in Council, with both his Hands whole, to the great confusion of his accusing *Arian* Enemies. Thereafter they produced an impudent Whore accusing *Athanasius* of Adultery with her, but *Athanasius* so convinced her in the face of the Synod, that she had not a word to answer: But *Eustathius* the Orthodox Bishop of *Antiochia*, him they accused also of Adultery with another impudent Whore, whom the *Arians* suborned, and she did swear it; and albeit the Innocent Bishop did constantly assert his innocence, yet they degraded him, and obtained

(*d*) Socrat. *lib.*2. *cap.*18.

tained at the *Emperour* to banish him; but thereafter, that wicked Woman (in the just Judgment of God) falling Sick, and dying in great bodily Torments, confessed her grievous sin of Perjury against Innocent *Eustathius*, and that the *Arians* had hired her with a Sum of Money. *(a)* *(a) Theodoret. lib.5. cap.21.*

A *fourth* instance of their deceit and subtilty, The *Arian* perceiving by more then 30. Years sad experience, that the Creed of that famous Council of *Nice* had given their cursed Cause a deadly wound, they craftily resolve to conveen a Council in that same City of *Nice*, and there write an *Arian* Creed to their own mind, and vent it for the old Orthodox *Nicen* Creed, and so to deceive the Vulgar: But He whose Throne is in Heaven, had them in derision; for when the *Arians* began to conveen in that City of *Nice*, the Lord sent a great Earthquake, which caused the *Arians* (with fear) flee out of the City: *(b)* But that Plot failing them, they hardened their Neck like an Iron Sinew, and with a Whores Forehead, persist in a like wicked Design; for, understanding that in *Thracia*, the next adjacent Country, there is a Town called *Nicea*, thither they hasten, and hold their Council, and conclude upon a blasphemous *Arian* Creed, deceitfully calling it the *Nicen* Creed.   *(b) Hieronimus ad annum domini 372.*

(c) Sozomen. lib.4. cap.15.

A *fifth* instance of their Falshood in these their many Councils, where Satan had his Throne, and Antichrist kept the Chair; They wrote nine several Creeds, not all confirming or explaining the former Creed, but some of them containing Contradictions, of which themselves were ashamed, *(d)* for a Liar should have a good Memory; yea, in the last of these Councils they ratifie their Council at *Seleucia* and its Creed, and cursed the Creed at *Ariminum*, because it was not Heterodox enough. *(e)*   *(d) Socrat. lib.2. cap.25.*

(e) Socrat. lib.4. cap.4.

As we have seen the Activity, Perfidity and Falshood of the *Arian* in spreading their Heresie, so in the fourth place we shall take a view of their Hellish Cruelty, practised against the Orthodox and true Church of God: For they poysoned (with their *Arianism*) the Emperour *Constantius*, who began his Reign *Anno Dom.* 336. and *Valence*, who began his Reign *Anno Dom.* 366. these two Emperours they instigate to raise cruel and bloody Persecution against the Orthodox during the time of their Empire, of which we shall only mention a few notable Instances.

First, The *Arians* at *Constantinople* raised a great Tumult of Sedition, that many Christians were troden under Foot to Death. (*a*)   (*a*) Socrat. *lib*.2. *cap*.9.

Secondly, The *Arian* Emperour *Constantius* having banished the Orthodox Bishop of *Constantinople*, the *Arians* strangled him in his Exile, and the Orthodox Bishop of *Adrianople* died in Prison with Torments. (*b*)   (*b*) Socrat. *lib*.2. *cap*.21.

Thirdly, Great Persecution was raised by the *Arians* in the Cities of the East against the Orthodox Christians, by Banishment, spoiling of their Goods, and sundry kinds of Torments. (*c*)   (*c*) Socrat. *lib*.2. *cap*.22.

Fourthly, The *Arians* at *Alexandria* upon the Lords Day invaded with Arms the Orthodox, and having kindled a great Fire, apprehended Orthodox Virgins (who, as they thought, would soonest yield to them,) these they threatned with Burning unless they turned *Arian*; but perceiving these holy Virgins Invincible Courage, resolute to die Martyrs for the Glory of the Sacred Trinity, they violently in the open Streets, pulled off all their Clothes, to put them to shame, and mocked them in their nakedness ; but these Virgins being of undaunted Courage to suffer for the Name of Christ, them the *Arians* so wounded on the Face, that their nearest Relations did hardly know them; and fourty Men they scourged with Rods, that some of them died, yet they refused to give their dead bodies to their Friends to bury ; and these who outlived their Scourging, part of them they Banished, of others not banished, the Chirurgians had great difficulty to pull out the Thorn Pricks out of their Flesh. At that same time, the *Arians* killed moe then thirty Orthodox Bishops in *Egypt* and *Lybia*, and banished sixteen moe, whereof some died in their cruel usage by the way, others died in the place of their Banishment; of which Martyrs the World was not worthy. (*d*)   (*d*) Socrat. *lib*.2. *cap*.23.

Fifthly, In *Constantinople* and the Country about, many Orthodox Bishops were banished by the *Arians*, and other of the Orthodox that refused to communicate with the *Arians* they cruelly tormented their Bodies, and then scobbing their Mouths, violently thrust in the sacramental Elements of the Lords Supper, and that not only of Men and Women, but also of Children; and these who were most reluctant they detained in Prison and Torments, that so the *Arian* intended by this

his

his work to get the honour that the Orthodox did communicate with them, but prophane forcing proved the *Arian* Communion to be the Table of Devils; yea, they thrust the Papes of some holy Women into a Chest, and closing its lid, cut off their Papes with a Saw, and others they burnt off their Papes with a red hot Iron. (*a*)   (*a*) Socrat. *lib*.2. *cap*.30. Theodoret. *lib*.2. *cap*.14.

Sixthly, The *Arians* in *Alexandria* conspired with the *Jews* and *Pagans*, and all three raised great Persecution against the true Christians there; they apprehended the holy Virgins, stripped them naked as they were born, and led them through the Streets, obscenely mocking them, and if any Beholder (in Christian compassion) did speak but one word in their favours, they were driven away with Wounds; thereafter, many of the Virgins they ravished, some they killed, and refused to give their Bodies to their Parents to be buried; yea, in this Tumult the *Arian* and *Pagan* committed so great abomination that I am ashamed to render them in *English*, (*b*) a most profane *Pagan* being a chief Actor of these Abominations, acted both in the Pulpit, and on the Altar of the chief Church of *Alexandria*; it was too like a Stage-Play of Satans divising against God's Word and Worship, the most profane the Devil could devise, and all this acted in the presence of the *Arian* Bishop, whom the *Pagan* Spokesman thus saluted, *O Bishop! who denies the Son of God, thy coming is welcome to us,* (*c*) *our god* *Serapis embraceth thee, and brought thee hither*; observe how well the (*b*) Theodoret. *lib* 4. *cap*.20. (*c*) Theodoret. *lib*.5. *cap*.22. Devil and the *Arian* does aggree, like Heart and Joy: This *Pagan* god *Serapis*, had a Church in *Alexandria* where he was worshipped, and in it a monstruous great Image, at that time much worshipped by the *Pagans* there. What true Christian can read the Perjury Falshood and hellish Cruelty of the *Arian*, and their atheistical profaning of the Lord's Supper, and not look upon them as incarnate devils, against these antichristian and profane bloody *Arians*, who blasphemed both the Son and Holy Ghost. The Orthodox Church were most zealous to defend the Truth, and for that cause, to sing the Doxology in their publick Worship, exactly according to the words of the Holy Scriptures: For then the *Arian* also keeped the singing of their own Doxology, but it was different from the Orthodox and Holy Scriptures. Now, considering the true Churches hard condition, when the *Arians* persecute them, and yet these holy Christians were most willing to suffer Martyrdom for the Name of Jesus, and also to sing the Doxology, therein professing their Faith in one God, in three Persons, Father, Son and Holy Ghost, equal in Power and Glory: Now, I would ask the

Christian now a days, If the Lord in His Providence did put them now in such a condition, to be persecuted to the death by the prevailing *Arian*, whether or not they would be content to suffer Martyrdom in defence of the honour of Christ, and also with the Orthodox Christian to sing the Doxology? would they both sing and suffer as these did, who are now singing triumphant Songs to Father, Son and Holy Ghost, having trode Satan and *Arians* under-foot; I willingly judge in Charity to these weak Lambs, they would then with the Orthodox Christians, both joyn in singing the Doxology, and also in suffering with them for the Name of Jesus; Then I ask them again, if they would have sung the Doxology if they had been going to the Stake to die in defence of the honour of Christ against the cursed *Arian*; then have they not as good reason and cause to sing Glory to the Father, Son and Holy Ghost, for His merciful Providence to them, who knowing their weakness better then themselves, hath preserved them from such an hour of temptation, and fiery tryal, not suffering them to be tempted above that they are able: But furthermore, I give you this warning, that if ye affirm with the three Children, you would sing in your fiery trial, but refuse to sing now when ye are preserved from it: Look to your selves that ye be not tempting God to cause you suffer *Arian* Persecution, that then ye may praise the glorious Trinity better, which now ye refuse, because the Lord frees you from *Arian* Persecution; this sore Trial the Lord avert.

2. In the last part of this Chapter, we shall observe the Testimony given by God and His Church in this fourth Century chiefly against the *Arian*; First, As for the true Church, they were not deficient to bear witness to the Truth, but as opportunity served, they conveened Orthodox Councils, and among others, one at *Sardica*, (a) of 370. Orthodox Bishops, where the *Arians* Accusations against *Athanasius* and other Orthodox Bishops were examined, and all found false and forged. Another Council at *Jerusalem*, (b) Anno Dom. 351. A third at *Millan* of 300. Bishops, (c) in which Councils they ratified the Orthodox Truth and *Nicen* Creed; and before that Anno Dom. 363. a Council of about 200. Bishops at *Ariminum* ratified the same Orthodox *Nicen* Creed.

(a) Socrat. *lib.*2. *cap.*16.

(b) Socrat. *lib.*2. *cap.*19.

(c) Theodoret. *lib.*2. *cap.*15.

As the Orthodox Church, during the time of the *Arian* Persecution, notwithstanding of all the cruelty used against them, the Church-men gave Testimony against the *Arian*, by Preaching, Writing, and Disputes, and both the Church-men and their Flocks by valiant suffering of Martyrdom;

The Doxology Approven. 19

tyrdom, and sealing the Truth with their Blood: So the Lord Himself from Heaven, divers ways did bear Testimony against the *Arian*, and for His Truth; first, in granting Signs and Wonders to be done by the Orthodox Church in this fourth Century, and in the *Arians* hottest Persecution, when in the mean time, the *Arians* had no Miracles amongst them, nor did they pretend to any; and although they had pretended to work Miracles, yet the *Arians* Miracles had been nothing but Satans lying Wonders: But God honoured even the persecute Orthodox to work glorious Miracles; for instance, the *Arians* having banished some Orthodox Christians to a remote Island in the Sea, where the *Pagans* worshipped the Devil, seated in a Grove, these banished Orthodox Christians first cast (a) out the Devil out of the *Pagan* Priests Daughter, then converted her and (a) Socrat. lib.4. cap.19. her Parents, and at last the whole *Pagans* of that Island to the Christian Faith. So the Devil could not stand before these Orthodox Christians.

A second instance, *Moses* an Orthodox Christian was famous for working of Miracles, who coming to *Alexandria*, refused to receive Consecration to a Bishoprick from *Lucius* Bishop of *Alexandria*, (b) (b) Socrat. lib.4. cap.29. because he was an *Arian*, but reproved him sharply, proving him to be altogether void of the true Principles of Christian Religion; but that same worker of Miracles received Consecration from the Orthodox Clergy to the said Bishoprick.

As the Lord did bear Testimony to the Orthodox Christians, and their Faith, by giving them the gift of Miracles, and not to the *Arian*, so did that Lord as Judge of the World declare and manifest His Wrath against the chief *Arian* Persecuters in this Century. First instance, *Constantius* the first *Arian* persecuting Emperour, who as he was false to God in turning *Arian*, so his kinsman *Julian* (whom he chused to be General of his Army) turned false to him; who having rebelled, *Constantius* leads an Army against him, but died by the way in *Silicia*, sore lamenting, and repenting of his *Arian* Heresie. (c) Second instance, The other *Arian* Emperour *Valence* was Satans evil Instrument, perverting the *Goths* to *Arianism*, (of which Poyson they were not cured some hundreds of Years therafter,) (d) and for the Emperours reward, the *Goths* rebelling, beat him and his Army in Battel, and he flying to a little

(c) Theodoret. lib.2. cap.32.

(d) Socrat. lib.4. cap.27.

Tower,

Tower, they burnt the Tower and him with Fire. (a) Third inftance, The Wrath of God was remarkable in the death of *George* the *Arian* Bifhop of *Alexandria*, (whofe cruelty is mentioned in this fame Chapter before, in the fixth inftance of the *Arian* Cruelty, where this *Arian George* was Ringleader,) for not many Years after the forefaid inftance of Perfecution, the *Pagans* in *Alexandria* raifed a feditious Tumult againft the faid *George*, pulled him out of the Church by the Ears, tied him to a Camel then did tear him in pieces, and burnt him and the Camel to Afhes. (b)

(a) Theodoret. *lib* 4. *cap.* 3. & Hieronimus *chronico ad annum* 382.

(b) Socrát. *lib.* 3. *cap.* 2.

CHAP. IV.

The unanimous practice and appointment of the univerfall Church, for finging of the Doxology, becaufe Satan and his fuppofts mad and ftupendious oppofition of the Doctrine of the Trinity, and fo warring againft God.

THe Glorious Trinity of Perfons in the God-head, being the great fundamental Article of our Chriftian Faith, and that Chrift is the Son of God, the fecond Perfon of the bleffed Trinity; upon which Rock the Chriftian Church is built, *Matth.* 16. 18. By which Name they are faved, *Acts* 4. 12 Even the great myftery of godlineffe, God manifefted in the Flefh, which Myftery cannot be known, nor believed aright to Salvation, unlefs we firft know and believe that the Son fent by, and from the Father, was incarnat, and not the Father, *John* 17. 3. To this point we have fpoken in the firft Chapter; Therefore Satan, in the three firft Centuries ftirred up moft Hereticks againft the Sacred Trinity, and the Incarnation of the Son of God, to which we have fpoken in the 2*d. Chapter*. Thirdly, The *Arians*, who rofe in the Fourth Century, being more Active and Subtil, Falfe, Bloody and prevalent, then any Hereticks which were before them, perfecuted the true Church of God, in an Hellifh manner, for this caufe, the then Orthodox Church, as they ufed many good means, for ftrengthening the Chriftians in the Faith, and confuting, confounding of Hereticks, as Preaching, Difputs, Writtings, Councils, and Church Cenfure, by Excommunication: all which Means, the God of Heaven Countenanced, and Bleffed with good Succefs: So in that Fourth Century, the True Church, in their Publick Worfhip did appoint, that at the clofe of finging the *Pfalm*, they fhould fing this Doxology, *Glory to the Father, to the Son, and to the Holy Ghoft,* in which Deed they have imitate the Lords own Example, commanding

ing *Moses*, *now therefore write ye this Song for you, and teach it the Children of Israel, put it in their mouths, that this Song may be a witness for me against the Children of Israel*, Deut. 31. 19. So the Primitive Church perceiving, by sad experience, Satans incessant malice, in stirring up Hereticks against the Sacred Trinity, and Mans Naturall weakness, and proneness to listen to Error, and believe Lies, especially against the blessed Trinity, most prudently and Piously aggreed, and unanimously to sing the Doxology to the blessed Trinity, in the publick Worship of God. to be a Witness against the *Arian*, and other Blasphemers of the Trinity, and for Confirmation of the Orthodox, and sound Believers in the True Faith, for Singing Glory to God, Father, Son, and Holy Ghost, being in it self, a Lawfull, and Holy unquestionable Duty of Christians, albeit there were neither Heretick to oppose, and Blaspheme, the Trinity, nor Devil to tempt them to that wicked Deed, then finding both wicked Men and Devils, by Experience, enemies to that sound and saving Truth, makes the singing of the Doxology, besides it's Lawfulness, and Expediency to be most usefull, and edifying for the People of God, and a strong preservative against Antitrinitarian Heresies.

Here we are not to think, that the Doxology, or praising of the Holy Trinity, was not used by the Doctors of the Church, these burning and shining Lights, before and beside the publick singing in the Church, for the Sacred Trinity being the great Fundamental of the Christian Faith, and object of Divine Worship, these Doctors ordinarily closed their Prayers, or Sermons, or other Writtings with the Doxology, *Anno Dom.* 165. *Policarpus*, Bishop of *Smirna* (who had been the Disciple, of the beloved Disciple, St *John*) dying a glorious Martyre, in presence of many thousand *Jews*, *Pagans* and *Christians*, ready to step into the Fyre, closed his heavenly Prayer thus, I glorifie thee through the everlasting high Priest Jesus Christ, thy welbeloved Son, to whom with the, and the Holy Ghost, be all Glory, Wo:ld without end, *Amen*. Here this blessed Martyr not only sealled the Doctrine of the blessed Trinity with his Death, but also the Blessed Glorious Trinity, Father, Son, and Holy Ghost Sealled that same Faith of this Faithfull Martyr with many miracles at his Death; of which we wrot in the second Chapter.(*b*) About the Year of Christ, 190. *Clemens Alexandrinus* writeth thus, Let us praise Father, Son, and Holy Ghost, who one, is all, and in whom are all, altogether Good, Beautifull, Wise, and Just, to whom be Glory, now and for ever. (*a*) In the Year of Christ 325. The famous Councill of *Nice*. having condemned *Arius*, and his Blaspheming Associats, for denying

(*b*) *Euf. lib.* 4. *hist. cap.* 19.

(*a*) *lib.* 3. *pædagog.*

ing the Co-eternity of the Son, and Holy Ghost with the Father, they writ a Synodical Letter to the Churches of *Alexandria*, *Ægypt*, *Lybia*, and *Pentapolis*; which they close with a Doxology to the Sacred Trinity, Thus, By the help of God, the Father Almighty, and our Lord Jesus Christ, with the grace of the Holy Ghost, to whom be glory for ever, *Amen*. (*b*)

The Synodical Epistle of the Council of *Illyricum* closeth thus; these things are inacted to the glory of the Father, Son, and Holy Ghost for ever.

Sozomen closeth the Preface to his Church History to Christ, with God the Father, and Holy Ghost be Glory for ever, *Amen*.

(*c*) *Macarius* a Church-man in *Ægypt*, who lived in the reign of *Constantine* and *Constantius*, closeth his 12th, 16th, and 17th. Homolies with the Doxology. About the Year of Christ 360. in the Church of *Antioch*, being a Patriarchall See at Publick Worship, were conveened most part Orthodox, but some *Arians* mixed with them, when they came to that part of the Worshhip, which a Chronologer (*d*) writes, was immediatly, after their singing the Psalm, then the Orthodox did sing the Doxology, Glory to the Father, and the Son, and the Holy Ghost, according to the Doctrine of the *Nicen* Council; But the *Arians* who were with them in the Church, differing from the Orthodox, sang Glory to the Father, by the Son, thereby purposing, that the Father was greater then the Son, which difference in the singing, being perceived by *Leontius* (*e*) then Bishop of *Antioch*, and inclining to *Arianisme*, putting his hand to his

(*b*) *Socrat. lib.* 1. *cap.* 6. *Theodoret lib.* 1. *cap.* 9.

δόξα καὶ προσκύνησις τῶ πατρὶ καὶ τῶ υἱῶ καὶ τῶ ἁγίω πνεύματι εἰς τὲς αἰῶνας-αμην, *Sozemen lib.* 3. *cap.* 19. πατέρα καὶ υἱὸν ὡς ὁμότιμον ἐδόξαζον κατα τὴν παράδοσιν τῆς ἐν νικαια συνόδε τον θεὸν ὑμνοῦντες.

(*d*) *Nicephorus, Hist. Ecclesiast. lib.* 9. *cap* 24. *Ait eos cecinisse Doxologiam ad finem Psalmodij.*

(*e*) *Leontius tametsi sordibus Arianæ blasphemiæ fuit inquinatus tamen eus callide admodum occultare studuit, Etenim cum clerum, & Laicam etiam multitudinem in duas partes divisam cerneret Orthodoxos adhibentes conjunctionem & Filio, & Spiritui Sancto, Arianus vero ante Filium* (Per.) *ante Spiritum Sanctum* (In.) *praponere; Ipse totam glorificationem tacitus secum recitavit adeo ut qui ei proximi; erant solum hanc particulam in secula seculorum audirent, hæc Theoretus, lib.* 2. *cap.* 24. *Ex Athanasio.*

Regnante Anastasio diuterius Arianorum Constantinop. *Episcopus cum quendam Barbam nomine baptizare intenderet, & spreta dominica institutione diceret baptizatur Barbas.* εἰς τὸ ὄνομα τε πατρος δι εἰς ἐν αγιο πνεύματι, *hoc dicto aqua in columbethra evanuit Barbas vera arrepta fuga exivit & miraculum*

Gray

Doxology Approven. 23

en this snow   *hoc cunctis significavit, Hæc scribit*
ll be much   *Theodorus lector in collect quæris lib.*
  Experience,   *2. & Nicephorus calisti, lib. 16.*
:, he did fore-   *hist. Eccles. cap. 35.*

Arian persecution of which I have spoken some-
of this Treatise, for the Orthodox did sing the
g to the Words of our Saviour in the Gospel,
Divine Institution of Baptisme, *Matth.* 28. 19. All
ner to the Father, and the Son, and the Holy
ian did sing Glory to the Father, by the Son,
where, observe, that the *Arian* as yet did not
sing the Doxology upon any pretended reason, or
ce as some men do now, but it is like the sing-
was then performed by the Orthodox with such
y, that the *Arian* was as yet afraid, or ashamed
the singing of it, as some now do.

who lived in the Year of Christ 369. in his Book
ly Ghost, *cap.* 27. He writs, that the most ancient
ds praise, to Father, Son, and Holy Ghost, ac-
d in Baptism, and these two great Doctors *Basil*
were contemporary Bishops in the Greek Church
: a Greek Leturgy, being their Mother tongue,
l at this day, in all the Christian Churches of the
thin the Greek

) The one Ly-   (a) In *Lyturgia*, St. *Basil* pro-
h Dayes (b)   pe finem καὶ σοὶ τὴν δόξαν καὶ
y on all other   εὐχαρισίαν καὶ προσκύνησιν ἀνα-
l in both these   πέμπομεν [ῶ πα]ρὶ καὶ]ῶ υἱῶ καὶ
:ology was, and   ]ῶ ἁγίω πνεύμα]ι νῦν καὶ ἀεὶ καὶ
oo Years with-   εἰς]ὲς αἰῶνας]ῶν αἰώροιν
teration (c)   (b) δόξα]ῶ πατρὶ καὶ]ῶ υἱῶ
n his sixth Or-   καὶ]ῶ ἁγίω πνεύμα]ι νῦν καὶ ἀεὶ
he Holy Ghost,   καὶ εἰς]ὲς αἰῶνας]ῶν αἰώων ἀμήν:
ither, Son, and   (c) προσκυνέω πά]ερα, καὶ
God-head and   υἱὸν καὶ πνεῦμα ἅγιον, τῶν μία
all glory honour   θεό]η]α τε καὶ δύναμιν,]ι αὐ]ῶ
er and ever A-   πᾶσα δόξα]ιμη κράτος εἰς]ὰς
     αἰῶνάς]ῶν αἰώνων ἀμήν.

Christ 370. St.
nasus, Bishop of
1e Churches of
he Father, Son,
s it was in the   (a) *Rome* 1. *Council.* pag.
, and for ever,   625. *editionis Parisiensis.*

F   be

be sung alwayes at the end of the Psalm.

(*b*) About the Year of our Lord 444. in the Council of *Vason*, an Act is made, because of the unbelief of *Arian* Hereticks.

Because not only in the Apostolick See, but also throughout all the East, and in all *Africk* and *Italy*, to guard against the deceit of Hereticks Blaspheming, that the Son of God was not ever with the Father, but began to be in time; therefore, in all their closings of singings in the publick Worship, after these Words, Glory to the Father, Son, and Holy Ghost in all these other Churches is added, as it was in the beginning, so we appoint that the same Words (as it was in the beginning) be mentioned in the Doxology in all our Churches also.

(*c*) Hence we may observe, That this addition (as it was in the beginning, was not first appointed at *Vason*, for their Act bears the contrare, that it was used in Churches far and near, before that time, which *Jeromes* desire to *Damasus* proves: But this Act at *Vason* gives the clear reason of the addition, viz. To guard the flock of Christ the better against *Arian* Hereticks, whereof some said there was a time when the Son of God was not.

Alexander Patriarch of *Alexandria*, one of the chief Fathers in the *Nicen* Council, to refute the *Arian*, brings that Text (*d*) among many others, *John* 1. 1. *In the beginning was the word, and the word was with God, and the word was God, by him all things were made,* and if he made all things, then he before the world, and also before that beginning, and consequently Eternal, as that Father reasoneth well, and St. *Basil* after him, for it were nonsense to say that there were priority of time in Eternity; For *Arius* said there was a time, when God was not a Father: Therefore the infallible Theologue of St. John began his Evangell with these

(*b*). *Concilium* Valense *provinciale sub Imperio* Theodosij *in moris cap.* 7. *cujus titulus ac propter hæreticorum incredulitatem post gloria, Patri,* &c. *sicut erat in principio,* &c. *semper dicatur, quia non solum in sede apostolica sed etiam per totam Orientem, & totam Africani vel Italiani propter Hæreticorum astutiam qui dei filium non semper fuisse, sed in tempore cæpisse blasphimant in omnibus clausulis post Gloria Patri, &c. sicut erat in principio,* &c. *dicatur, etiam & nos universis Ecclesiis nostris ita dicendum esse decrevemus.*

(*c*) *Symbolium Nicenium in fine.* Τὰς δὲ λέγοντας ἦν ποτὲ ὅτε οὐκ ἦν υἱὸς τοῦ θεοῦ ——— Τελες ἀναθεματίζει ἡ καθολικὴ καὶ ἀποστολικὴ τῶν ἐκκλησία.

(*d*) *Socrat. lib.* 3. *cap.* 3.

words

words, intending in his Gospel, to assert Christs God-head against two abominable Hereticks in his time. *Ebion* and *Cerinthus* at whom *Arius* had learned his Blasphemies, and from this same Text, *Calvin* refutes both the old *Arian* and *Servetus* a vile Blasphemer, his own contemporary, who was burnt at *Genevah*, for a most blasphemous Heretick. In the Year of Christ 627. in the third Council of *Toledo*, consisting of the Church-men of *Spain*, and *Galatia* inact, whosoever sayes not Glory to the Father, and the Son, and the Holy Ghost let him be accursed; by saying they mean singing, For then four hundred years before that, the Doxology was sung in all the Temples of the universal Church. And so in this Council, all of them in the close of the same, in the praises of God, they cryed, Glory to the Father, and the Son, and the Holy Ghost, as the Learned may read in the Tomes of Councils, by this cursing mentioned in this Councill, It appears, they judged, that no Orthodox Christian would refuse to sing the Doxology, they did not imagine any will refuse except a Heretick.

In the Year of Christ, 633, in the Fourth Councill of *Toledo*, there are some accused, for rejecting the Sacred Hymnes composed by *Hilary* and *Ambrose* two famous Saints, and being received, and used in the Churches, yet these Men refused to sing them, because they were not in the *Holy* Scripture, for which refusal they were Excommunicat, yet these same very Men, did not scruple nor refuse to sing the Doxology, which was then constantly sung in the Church, at the close of every *Psalm*: Hence it is probable, that these men who refused to sing the Churches *Holy* Hymnes, and were willing to sing the Doxology, did estimat it of a higher rank, and counted it in with Divine and Spirituall Songs.

(*a*) The Learned have observed, that the *Arian* persecution which was in this Fourth Century, was more bitter to the Souls of the Saints, and true Christians, then the Suffering during the ten Persecutions, in the first 300. Years, from *Pagan* Emperours: for then the Christian Martyrs received their Crown of Martyrdome from their Lord in Heaven, with acclamations of praise from all their contemporary Christians without all malignant murmure, or obloquie; which was a sharp spur to hasten Christians to run that race; for ingenuous spirits know what humane applause will do even to the godly, to encourage them

(*a*) διόπερ ἐγὼ πέπεισμαι μείζονα ὑμῖν, &c. *Quocirca ut mea fert sententia major merces & præmium potius apud justum indicem reponitur quam veteribus illic martyribus cum illi in confessa positum reportarent martyrij apud homines existimationem & laureolas à Deo acceperint suas vobis autem desint in certamine pari à populo collati honores*, Basil *tom.* 2. *Epist.* 303. *pag.* 1074.

them to a good action, and rouse them up to their Duty, even allowed by God, *Phil.* 4. 8. Whatsoever things are of good report, if there be any vertue, and if there be any praise think on these things: But in this fourth Century, the Christian suffering Persecution, and Death it was not from *Pagans*, but from these that called themselves Christians, even the *Arian*, who being prevalent, and putting to Death the Orthodox Christians, yet the *Arian* cryes out, these are not true Christians, but we; they are justly suffering Death for Errors in Christianity; Therefore writs the Learned, that the Martyrs in the fourth Persecution their reward will be greatest in Heaven.

And because this Persecution was so much the sadder to the Orthodox Christian, and in this Century, the King of Saints, who promised His presence to His Church on Earth, seemed to be asleep, like that *Matth.* 8. 24. while the Ship is filled with waves: yet in the mean time, though thus he had decreed, to let His brittle Vessel, and His Disciples suffer a Storm, yet therefore he provided two excellent Pilots in this Century, and indued them with so great a measure of Piety, Learning undaunted Courage, and Prudence, that the one succeeding to the other, in the Eastern Church, where the *Arian* Storm did most rage; by Dispute, and Writing, and couragious Sufferings, they faced the Enemy, and kept the Flock of Christ together. *Athanasius* Patriarch of *Alexandria*, and after him *Basil* Archbishop of *Cæsarea*, both which keep the Styl of Great, untill this day; for they got it, because of their worth, *Athanasius*, even from the *Arian* Emperour *Constantius*, and *Basil* from the Apostat Emperour *Julian*: As is to be seen in both their Letters of record, with St. *Basils* Letters of sharp rebuke, which did become a pious Bishop to *Julian* an Apostat.

As for the *Arian*, as ye read in this Chapter before, in singing of the Doxology, shuned to sing it according to the Scriptures, Glory to the Father, and to the Son, and to the Holy Ghost, but by the Son in the Holy Ghost, which was a deceitfull Invention, and the Church History tells us the thing it self, but does not unfold the intrigue and mystery of it; which St. *Basil* hath done at full length; for that their singing in that their new devised way, was a subtil trick of the Devil, for under it they couched their Error, and Blasphemy; only giving Glory to God the Father, and for the Son, considering him only as the Fathers Instrument, but not equal with Him in Glory, and far less the Holy Ghost, which depths of Satan are found out by St. *Basil*, to the shame of the *Arian*, of which he writs at large, which the Learned do read. (*a*) And that they were so obstinat in their Errors, that nothing could prevail to gain them to sing the Doxology

(*a*) *Basil tomo* 2. *lib. de spiritu sancto contra Arianus cap.* 2, 3, 4, 5. and 25. *cap.* 7. 10.

according

The Doxology Approven.   27

according to the Scriptures, *(b)* That they would as soon quite their tongue, as quite that form of Doxology, which they used: where St. *Basil* grants, that their way of singing the Doxology might be exponed in an Orthodox sense according to the Scriptures; but was not to be suffered in these Hereticks, because it was well known they sang them in an Heretical and Blasphemous sense, against the Son and Holy Ghost.

(b) *lib. de spiritu sancto. cap. 25. ἀλλὰ τὰς γλώσσας, ἂν πρόοιντο μᾶλλον ἢ τὴν φωνὴν ταύτην δέξαιντο καὶ, scilicet isti citius abjecerent linguas quam hanc vocem recipiant: & idem cap. 25. Doxologiam Ariani recitat tibi Patri honor & gloria per unigenitum filium tuum in spiritu sancto, qui sermo nunc usitatior est istis ipsa, ut ita loquar respiratione, & cap. 29. in oriente Orthodoxi dignoscunt suos ab* Arianis *signo Doxologiæ.*

Yet reflecting upon the *Arian* practice, observe, that they did choise it as a less evil, and scandal to sing the Doxology with some change of the short syllabes of interjections, conjunctions then not to sing it at all; For to have refused the singing of it, had been a shorter cut; but the reason was, publick shame would not suffer them altogether to seperat from the Orthodox Church, in that so unquestionable a duty, and so well known a part, of the Christians publick worship, then let these in *Scotland*, who call themselves Orthodox, and refuse altogether to sing the Doxology, either one way or other, see to it, and I beseech them to commune with their own hearts, and smit upon their own Breast, and amend.

They who are pleased to read the History of the *Arian* Persecution in this fourth Century, will perceive the true Church of Christ at a very low ebb, and under one of the greatest eclipses that ever it suffered since the two Disciples said, *we trusted that it had been He,* Luk. 24.21: and the eleven Apostles were weeping in secret, Mark 16. 10. yet the Lord who brought *David* out of his Deeps, and *Daniel* out of the Lions Den, and the three Children out of the seven times hotter Furnace, *Jonah* out of the Whales belly, and *Lazarus* out of the grave, and commanded the dry scattered Bones to stand up a strong Army, Ezek. 37.10: and in the beginning, commanded Light to shine out of Darkness, and bringeth Good out of Evil, out of the Churches Persecution and low condition, brought the more glory to His own Name, and more strength of Faith to His Church, whereby the *Arians* ungodly way of proceeding when they got the Power in their hand, they declared to the World what they were, even not the true Church of Christ, but the Seed of the Serpent, promoting their Religion by Injustice and Perjury, the Children of *Abaddon* and *Apollyon*, that Liar and Murderer from the beginning, *John* 8. 44. promoting their hellish Religion by cruel tormenting and murdering of the Orthodox, they being the first that usurped ed the name of Christian, withall, intending to propagate their Religion with Fire and Sword, which is not Christs way, nor of His true Christians, but of Antichristians; and therefore in persecuting of the true Church, as they had learned it at the *Pagans*, who lived before them, so they were glad to take the help of the *Pagans* who lived with them; therefore the Lord at last brought the *Arian* to confusion, and put their lying Lips to silence, so that ever thereafter, they were hated and abhorred, and despaired ever to prevail any more as they had done. The second Good which the Lord brought out of this Evil, was the perfite setling of the Christian Faith, the Lord bestowing on the Orthodox such Courage to suffer, such Faith and Constancy, and heavenly Joy, that the *Arian* was confounded thereby; yea, and while the Orthodox were suffering for the Glory of God and His Truth, the Lord from Heaven did approve and seal His Truth which they believed and professed, even making them His Instruments to work glorious Miracles; but in the mean time the *Arian* wrought no Miracle, nor so much as pretended to work any lying Miracle, as *Jannes* and *Jambres* did against *Moses*, to the hardning of *Pharaoh*; wherein I observe the Lord's wonderful Providence to over-ruling the *Arian*, that they did not so much as mint to a Miracle, whereas the Miracles of the Orthodox Church were undenyable, and thus the Lord from Heaven did dicide the Contraversie betwixt the *Arian* and the Orthodox in favours of His Church, and this the Lord's doing did so confirm them in the true Faith of the blessed Trinity, that the gates of Hell ever since was not able so to brangle it, and also His Church which had used the Doxology to the blessed Trinity in their publick Worship before that time, was now more confirmed in their Practice, and resolute to make use of it without fail ever thereafter, especially in the publick Worship.

In this Chapter at Page 24. we spoke anent the addition put to the Doxology, mentioned in the Council of *Vauson* (*as it was in the Beginning.*) If some object that that addition is obscure, and does not clearly assert the Eternity of the Trinity before the World began, as (*for ever*) in the close of the Doxology asserts the Eternity of the Trinity for ever after the World: I answer, we have proven indenyably from the Church History, that these words (*as it was in the Beginning*) in the Doxology are taken from the first Chapter and first Verse of St. *John*'s Gospel, which words, the Holy Ghost there made use of, to assert the Co-eternity of the Son with the Father, and therefore that same Text was used by the Fathers of the *Nicen* Council against *Arius*, who denied the preceeding Eternity of the Son with the Father; and the Fathers of the Council of *Syrmium* against the *Arians* writ, that *Ebion* and *Cerinthus* who were blasphemous Hereticks in the days of the Apostle St. *John*, denied the Godhead of the Son, and consequently his Co-eternity with the Father: And therefore as the scope of all St. *John*'s

John's Gospel is chiefly to prove Christ's Godhead against these two Hereticks, so albeit that first Proposition, *in the Beginning was the Word*, taken alone, by way of separation from the following words, will not prove any Eternity or Co eternity with the Father; yet joyn it in coherence with the following words, and that will clear the right Sense of this Beginning in the first of *John*, and the Beginning mentioned in the Doxology, and ye will find it the same in Sense with the first words in holy Writ, *Genes.* 1. 1. *In the beginning God made Heaven and Earth*; and the same work of Creation is here attribute to the Son, in the third following Verse, all things are made by Him, &c. so that the Sense of these words *in the Beginning*, both in the beginning of *Genesis*, and beginning of *John*'s Gospel, is clearly this, as from the Beginning was the Word, and that Word was God, so is now and ay shall last; And as in the Beginning all things were made by Him, and so He was Eternal before the World that He made in the beginning of Time, as in the beginning of *Genesis* God was Eternal before the making of the World, for to take any single Proposition in Scripture, and admit no Sense to it but that which that one single separate Proposition will afford, and so admit no further clearing of its Sense from antecedent and consequent Scriptures. The Fathers and Doctors of the Church have ever made that practice the mark of a Heretick, or at best of a heretical and contentious Spirit, so that the meaning of the words, *as it was in the Beginning*, compared with the rest of the Verse, *In the beginning was the Word, and the Word was God*, is as much in Sense, as if the Doxology had said, as it was from Eternity is now and ay shal last.(a)

(a *Vide sis* Basil *in Tomo primo, in locum*, 1 John 1. Prov. 8. 23.

CHAP. V.

The cause of the continuance of the Doxology in after Ages, viz. The continuance of the Churches Persecution, and Temptation from Arians, and other Blasphemers of the Trinity, as Eutichians within, and Mahumetanes without the Church; and the Rise and Growth of the Socinian Heresie, notwithstanding Gods witness against them, and the Church and Magistrats endeavours in many Kingdoms, these Blasphemous Antitrinitarian Hereticks, remained and nested with Anabaptists and Quakers, all three Blasphemous Antitrinitarian Hereticks, which gives sufficient cause for the continuance of the Doxology:

IN this fifth Chapter I intend to give a brief account of the Molestation and Persecution that the Church of Christ suffered from the remnant of *Arians*, and other *Antitrinitarian* Blasphemers, beginning at

30 *The Doxology Approven.*

at the fifth Century, and continued to this very present time; therefore I divide it in two parts, The first containing the *Antitrinitarians* for 1000. Years, even to the sixteenth Century; The second part containing a list of the chief *Socinians, Quakers*, and others who deny the Sacred Trinity. In the beginning of the fifth Century, the great Tempest of the *Arian* Power and Persecution was much abated in the Mercy of God, who *will not suffer the rod of the wicked to ly always on the lot of the Righteous, lest the Righteous put forth their hand to iniquity*, *Psal.* 125. 3. And among the many other means used by the Church against these blasphemous Heresies, the Lord blessed that mean, especially of the Churches Councils, especially these General Councils of *Nice, Ephesus, Constantinople* and *Chalcedon,* which (as *Beza* well characterizeth them) holiest Meet-

ings the Sun saw since the days of the Apostles, who proved (against these Blasphemers) terrible as an Army with Banners, and like a Rock on the Sea shore that breaks all the Waves that violently beat upon it, but it self remains whole and immovable, (a) for why, the Christian Faith of these General Councils was built upon the Rock, against which the Gates of Hell shall never prevail, *Mat.* 16. 18.

(a) Beza *Epist.* 81. *Amplissimus ille* Nicenæ, Ephisinæ, Chalcedonensis, *Synodi concessus; quo nihil unquam sanctius nihil Augustius ab Apostolorum excessu Sol unquam aspexit, qui putat fundamentum omnis Religionis, id est veri Dei cognitionem maximos illos, & præstantissimos angelos Dei non tenuisse, sane indignus est qui in Ecclesia Dei sentiatur.*

In this fifth Century and some following, not only the *Arians* were not altogether extinct, but still remained a Prick in the side of the true Church, especially these barbarous Nations, who were not under the command of the Christian Emperours, to wit, *Goths* and *Vandals*, who were turned *Arians*, and persecuted the true Church so far as they had Power or Opportunity.

Secondly, In the midst of this Century arose another sort of Hereticks called *Eutichians*, Blasphemers against Christ, who vexed the true Church about 300. Years, and sometimes were cruel Persecuters. (b)

(b) Beza, *Itidem exercuit Ecclesiam crassissimum illud* Eutichis *delirium annos plusminus trecentos, subinde interpolatis, & novo quodam fuco oblitis erroribus renascens.*

Before the *Arian* and *Eutichian* Hereticks were crushed, Satan stirred up the *Mahumetans*, who are professed Blasphemers of the Sacred Trinity.

In the Year of Christ 441. The *Vandals* in *Africk* being *Arians*, put to death the Orthodox Christians by cruel Torments. (c)

(c) Prosper. *in chronico.*

Anni

Anno Christi 447. Arose a mad Monk, who falsly taught the mixing together of Christ's two Natures, and so destroying them both, he was condemned by a General Council at *Chalcedon*, of 630. Bishops, *Anno Domini* 451. This Heresie continued the longer, and prevailed the more, because of two Emperours *Anastatius* and *Heraclius* favourers of the same. (d)

(d) Evagrius *lib.2§5. & cap.8. & cap.10. & lib.3. cap.5. add 22. & lib.4. cap.9, & 10.*

Anno 489. Many Orthodox Bishops in *Africa* were banished by the *Arians* who were prevalent there. (e)

(e) Palmerius *in chron.*

Honoricus King of the *Vandals*, *Arians* in *Africk* banished more then 400. Orthodox (f) Bishops, some he burnt to Ashes, and some of them their Tongues were pulled out, who flying to *Constantinople*, spoke miraculously as if they had had Tongues. (g)

(f) Antonius *chronica, parte 2.*

(g) Evagrius *lib.4. cap.14, & 15.*

Anno 448. The *Eutichians* in *Alexandria* slew the Orthodox Bishop *Proterius* in the Church, harled his body throgh the Streets, and gnashed his Bowels with their Teeth. (a)

(a) Evagrius *lib.2. cap.8.*

Anno 496. Many *Manicheans*, who also were Blasphemers of the blessed Trinity, were detected at *Rome*, and their Books burnt.

Honoricus King of the *Vandalls*, in *Africk*, being *Arian*, banished at once 5000. Orthodox Christians. (b)

Anastasius the Emperour, *Anno Dom.* 520. Commanded not a Trinity; but a Quaternity to be worshipped, he was smitten with a thunder bolt, and so dyed in his wicked Reign, 300. Orthodox were killed, and some Orthodox Bishops banished (c)

(b) *Centuria Magdeburgensis*

(c) *Petrus Diaconus & Platina.*

(d) *Theodoricus Arian* King of the *Gothes* in *Italy* persecuted the Orthodox there, and the King of the *Arian Gothes* in *Spain* slew his own natural Son for turning Orthodox.

(d) *Centuria Magdburgensis Centuria 6. cap. 8.*

(e) The *Gothes* in *Spain*, who had long persecut the Orthodox Christian, they were at last converted

(e) *Magdeburgensis Centuriæ centuria 6. cap. 9.*

converted to the true Faith *Anno* 585.

In the seventh Century, the *Monothelites*, which were a Branch of the *Eutichian* Heresie troubled the true Church, for the Emperour *Constance* was a *Monothelite*, and also *Heraclius Arjovaldus* King of *Lambards* was an *Arian*, Anno Dom. 640.

Rotharius another of their Kings was *Arian* also, in the seventh Century; beside the trouble that the Church endured from the *Eutichian*, and *Monotholite* Hereticks, which were chiefly in the Eastern Church at *Constantinople*, and *Alexandria*, so be the *Arians* in *Italy*.

In this Century arose *Mahumet*, and composed his *Alcaran*, Anno Dom. 622. In which Blasphemously they deny the blessed Trinity; These not only spread, and prevailed mightily in *Asia*, and *Africk*, but also crossed the *Hellespont*, and molested *Greece*, both with the Sword, and Blasphemies; yea, also they crossed the Mediterranian over against *Spain*, and *Italy*, at last, Anno Dom. 829. came over with a Navy, from the Coast of *Barbary*, and spoiled *Rome*, and returned to *Africk* with the Prey, and again, Anno Dom. 845. (f) came over and spoiled *Rome* the 2d. time, and Anno Dom. 933. came over the third time, and spoiled *Genoa*.

(f) *Palmerius* in *chronico*.

In the 7th Century, the Orthodox Church gave Testimony against Hereticks, In a Council held at *Rome*, Anno Dom. 650. of a 100 Bishops, and upward, where the *Monotholites* and the *Antitrinitarians* were condemned, and another there of 125. Bishops, and a third at *Constantinople*, Anno. Dom. 681. of 150. Bishops.

And as the true Church gave Testimony against the *Antitrinitarian* Hereticks, so the Lord from Heaven, by His signal Judgements; For First, *Honoricus* King of *Vandalls* in *Africk*, an *Arian*, and cruel persecuter of the Orthodox, was long tormented with Venemous Boils; at last was consumed with Worms, and so ended his wretched Life.

Secondly, in this same Century, *Theodoricus* King of the *Gothes* in *Italy* a vile *Arian*, having murdered an Orthodox Noble Man Senatour, named *Symachus*, thereafter shortly sitting at Table, the head of a great Fish dressed in a Dish set before him, which he imagined to be the head of *Symachus*, and was so stupified, that he dyed with fear.

Abaliardus, a professor in *Paris*, about the year 1143. wrot Blasphemously against the blessed Trinity, whom *Bernard* refuted, and then there conveened a Council of Church-men in *France*, where he was confuted, convinced, converted (a)

(a) *Caranza folio* 258.

The Doxology Approven. 33

In the Year, 1215. In the Council of *Lateran*, Joachim *Abbas* his Erronious Book against the Trinity, was condemned, to which he submitted *(b)*   *(b) Caranza folio 250.*

If it be objected, that seing, in the Church History, and Councils, from the seventh Century to the fifteenth, there is only mention of two *Antitrinitarian Hereticks*, and consequently these Blasphemous Heresies being now banished, and buried; and seing it is granted, that the Doxology was first appointed to be sung in the Church, by occasion of *Antitrinitarian Hereticks*, for confirming in the Faith, the Lords People against their Blasphemies, why then was it any longer continued after the cause was removed? I answer, because the Church then perceived, by comfortable experience, that the constant singing of the Doxology in the Publick Worship of God, had proved an excelent mean, to confirm Christians in the Doctrine, and Faith of the Trinity, and to guard them against the temptations of Satan, and his supposts, and their own corruption, who were all yet lying in wait, to blow at the Ashes of the little spunks of the said old Blasphemies, that seemed to be buried many hundred years before. This is *Calvins* Metaphore, and accordingly it came to passe, for in the year of Christ 1531. Satan did fill the heart, and furnished the pen of a *Spaniard Servetus* with the Blasphemies, and black Venome of that Old Serpent. and now we intend to begin the 2d. Part of this Chapter, and to manifest to every Christian Reader, that if the universal Church had good cause to appoint the singing of the Doxology because of the Blasphemies of the *Arians* against the Sacred Trinity: So now in this old and doting Age of the World, the Church have much cause to continue that ancient practice, for the new, and late opposers of this blessed Trinity in this Age, are more blasphemous then ever the old *Arian* was, of which the rise and growth in *Europe*, we intend to give you a summar account:

First, That *Spaniard Servetus* being a Physician by profession, travelled 30. Years in *Pole*, *Hungary*, and *Transalvania*, practising Medicine, but infecting Souls with his Blasphemies (a worse disease then all his Bodily Cures) For which he was first apprehended, and imprisoned at *Lions* in *France*, but escaped Prison there, afterward having written some Books against the Sacred Trinity, he was apprehended at *Geneva*, for his Blasphemies, and obstinancy in them, was condemned by the Magistrat, and burnt quick, *Anno Dom*. 1553.

(a) Genevas just punishing of him, is approven by the *Cantons* of *Tygurie* *(b) Scaffusium (c)* *Melancton*, and *(d) Æcolampadius* refuts him, and *Calvin* also, in his *Institutiones*, & *Opuscula*, and

(a) Beza Epist. 81.
(b) Calvin. Epist. 157.
(c) Calvin. Epist. 158.
(d) Calvin. Epist.

Mel-

34 The Doxology Approven.

Melancthon in his Fourth Volumne, who, in the Year, 1556. writ͛ to the *Vesalians* vulgo the *Veisle*, that if any maintained *Servetus* Errors, he should be expelled out of their Town: and Cardinal *Hosius* one of the three, that presided in the Council of *Trent* in his Works, folio, 352. Writs, that *Servetus* justly deserved so to die for his Blasphemies, and *Beza* gives a just, but black Testimony of him. (*e*)

(*e*) *Beza Epist.* 81. *In unico Serveto revocati sunt ab inferes Somasatenus, Arius & Eutiches, Marclon & Apollinaris, quod ibidem erudite probat inductione comparativa.*

Servetus, having strongly fermented four Disciples; to wit, *Valentinus, Gentilis, Alciat* of *Milan, Gibradus,* and *Blandrata. First, Valentinus* spread his Errors secretly in *Geneva*, for which, being taxed, renunced them under his own hand, under pain of perjurie; notwithstanding began to spread them the second time; for which he was imprisoned, and to be liberat from Prison, wrot a second Recantation of his Blasphemies; and at the command of the Magistrat, burnt them publiekly with his own hands: Thereafter spread his Errors in *France*, and *Italy. Arius* was but once perjured, but he twice; then he went to *Pole*, where he did meet with *Blandrata* and *Alciat* his old Companions; which two had also fled out of *Geneva*; and these three spread their Errors in *Pole* two years, untill the King of *Pole* banished them out of his Dominions; then *Gentilis* wandered through *Austria, Moravia* and *Savoy*, at last was apprehended within the confines of the Republick of *Bern*, and for his doubled perjury, and obstinancy in his Blasphemies against the blessed Trinity, was judicially condemned at *Bern* by the Magistrat, and burnt in the Year of Christ, 1556. (*a*) The History whereof is written at length, by *Aritius* Professor at *Bern*.

(*a*) Bucan. *loco* 1. *quest. Sect.* 5. Beza *epist.* 81.

Third *Blandrata* a Physician, disput often against *Calvin* at *Geneva*, thereafter in *Germany, Helvetia* and *Pole* vented his Errors, at last turned *Arian, Anno Dom.* 1569. and wrot against the Trinity, *Faustus Sosinus* in his Book of Epistles, *pag.* 687. calls *Blandrata* his great Patron, to be ever in honour with him, but at last *Blandrata* was suffocat in his bed by his own brother son, and died (*b*) miserably.

(*b*) *Beza epist.* 81.

The Fourth *Alciot* turned *Mahumitan*, and fled to *Turkie.* (*c*)

(*c*) *Beza epist.* 16:

Gilbraldus died of the Pestilence, *Beza* writes of other two, whereof the one drowned himself in a well.

The other *Ochinus*, how miserable he died, all *Pole* knew, as writs *Beza*, and Cardinal *Hosius*.

Stan-

The Doxology Approven: 35

Stancarus in *Pole* wrot against the Sacred Trinity, which the Orthodox Synod in *Pole* condemned, and the Divines of *Hidelberg*, and *Tigurie* refuted, and *Calvin* also, *An. Dom.* 1563. and *Beza* 1568. (d) *An.* 1567 a Book written at *Aiba Julia* by (d) *Beza epist. ad Polonos* 28. the Hereticks in *Sarmatia* and *Transilvania* is refuted at large, by *Zanchius de tribus Elohim*, *Georgius Paulus*, Superintendent of the Hereticall Churches in the Dioces of *Croco*, of whom writs *Beza* Epist. 81.

Statorius against whom *Beza* writs Epist. 15, and 16.

Andrew Duditbius, sometime a Bishop in *Hungarie*, and a conspicuous member of the *Trent* Council, he left the *Roman Church*; to him *Beza* writs his first Epist. *Anno Dom.* 1570. both large and loving, yet at last he fell in the snare of the *Transilvanian Hereticks*.

Sylvanus Pastor in *Hydelberg* turns *Arian*, and Traitor against his Prince *Palatine*; For these two crymes, he was beheaded, *Anno Dom.* 1522. His Colleague *Menzerus* escaping out of Prison, went first to *Pole*, then to *Transilvania*, at last to *Constantinople*, and there turned a circumcised *Turke*; he dyed crying, and roaring most terribly, that the *Turks* said, they never saw such a fearfull death, and that he was a Child of Satan; and the Reader may think no wonder of his desperat death, seing he had renounced his Saviour, and Baptisme.

Sedelius in *Pole* denyed Christs Divine Nature, and the New Testament.

Lelius Sosinus an *Italian*, foresaking the Errors of the *Roman-church*, *Calvine* wrot an Epistle to him, *Anno Dom.* 1555. of him *Beza* writs Epist. 81.

Faustus Socinus, his Nephew leaving *Italy*, came to *Tyguri*, with his Uncles Papers, where he spent three years in privat Studies, he was of a quick wit, but too proud, and bold, he confesseth in his writs, that he had little Logick, Greek, or Hebrew, he went to *Transilvania*, and there spread his Errors, he was in such repute with these Hereticks, that even at this day they are designed *Socinians*.

Franciscus Davidis: about the Year 1580. Superintendent in *Transilvania*, to that Sect of Hereticks, denyed that Christ was God, or the Messias, or should be worshipped; For which the Prince of *Transilvania* cast him in Prison, where he turning mad, dyed in dispair, affirming he saw the Devils came to take him away with them.

Poltelogus a *Dominican* at *Rome*, , fled to *Poland*; turned *Arian*, but was brought back to *Rome*, and burnt.

Smalcius Socinian Preacher at *Racovia*, wrot a large *Socinian* Catechism, Printed, *Anno Dom.* 1608. As *Socinus* had written another, and still the *Socinians* are busie scribling their Blasphemies, and Printing them, as *Goslavius*, *Anno Dom.* 1613. And *Nicolaides Anno. Dom.* 1614.

An

An Advocat at *Paris*, *Anno Dom.* 1616. caused Print *Abailardus* his Blasphemies, which had been condemned, and accursed, by a Church Council, above 500. years before.

Anno Dom. 1620. *Servetus* Books were turned in Dutch, and Printed in *Belgia* in which he blasphemes the most blessed Trinity. (*a*)

(*a*) *Triceps cerberus diabolicum phantasma & illusio:*

Doctor *Forbes*, *Anno Dom.* 1631. refutes a dissertation of a certain *Socinian* then newly written. (*b*)

(*b*) *Instructionum historico Theologicarum, lib.* 1. *cap.* 7.

Anno Dom. 1642: *Crellius*, *Socinian* Preacher at *Racovia*, hath Printed a Book against the Trinity, and after him, *Stychmanus*.

The *Socinians* not only increased in *Pole*, and *Transilvania*, but also are come to *Belgia*, where they consort with the *Arminian*, For *Anno Dom.* 1611. The Orthodox Synod in *Pole* writs to *Paraeus*, regrating, that the *Socinians* in *Pole* made much of *Arminius*; and now the later *Arminians* are poysoned with *Socinianism*, as is clear from the writtings of *Episcopius* their Chiftain. (*c*) It was granted indeed, that the *Socinians* are banished *Belgia* by publick Proclamation of the States of the *Natherlands*, yet notwithstanding, many *Socinians* lurk there, under the notion of *Remonstrants*, and *Anabaptists*, both which Sects are tolerat there, and who all three joyn, and agree in many of their Opinions, as writs *Hoorn Beek*, Divinity Professor at *Utright*, *Anno Dom.* 1650.

(*c*) *Socinanismi confutati tom.* 1. *pag.* 92.

(a) *Anno Dom.* 1638. *Sartorius* a *Socinian* at *Amsterdam* wrot a Letter to *Adam Frank Socinian* Preacher at *Claudiopolis*, which the Prince of *Transilvania* intercepted, and caused Print, where is written, that in *Holland* there is a great harvest of *Socinians*. (*a*)

The *Socinians* do not only lurk, and multiply in *Belgia*; but which is lamentable, are creept over to *England*, Mr. *Edwards Gangrene parte prima*, Printed at *London*; *Anno Dom.* 1645. Writs, That here the Doctrine of the Trinity by too, too many is called a Popish Tradition, and part. third

(*a*) Voetius *de tolerantia Antitrinitariorum ministri remonstrantes non pauci in* Socinianis *erroribus deprehensi inter quos celebres* Hendricus Slatius Adolphus Venator Gesterani *duo, & complures in* Zuid. Hollandia. *Ann. Dom.* 1618. *& * 1619. *Idem* Voetius *in thesebus de necessitate, & utilitate dogmatis de trinitate scribit, quod Remonstrantes inter suos tolerent, foverent, promoveant eos omnes quos* Socinianis *aut* Anabaptisticis *Erroribus, aut pejoribus opinionibus delibutos, probe noverint* E. G. Velfingium, Tonbergium.

pag.

pag. 58. Thus he writs, all men may see, that many in *England* are *Arians*, and *Antitrinitarians*, he writs also, *pag.* 136. a Letter from Holland to London, dated 1646. Here we burn the Books of the *Socinian* Errors, and they dare not be sold in these parts; but at *London*, is taught Blasphemy against God, and his Christ: and a Minister in *Holland*, wrot a Letter, dated *October* 18. 1646. to some Ministers in *London*, that diverse English Merchants were seeking to buy *Socinus* Works, and *Crellius*, &c. from a Stationer in *Holland*; and when the Stationer answered, that these Books were prohibit by the States Generall, the Merchant replyed, neverthelesse you may transport them from other Nations, and we shall give you for them what you will, and the Generall Assembly in *Scotland, Anno Dom.* 1648. *Seff.* 43. Writs thus, *Socinianisme* is now spread in *England*. As for our sentiment upon the *Socinian*, there was in the ancient Church two Heresies, that were most dangerous, and prevalent; First, the *Arian*, then the *Pelagian*, both which the Orthodox Church zealously opposed, and justly condemned; but the late *Socinian* hath drunk in all the poyson both of the *Arian* and *Pelagian*, and much more.

Secondly, That as the Ancient Church did condemne *Arius*, and *Pelagius* in their Councils, and being obstinat, Excommunicat them: So the Ancient Fathers (b) denyed the *Arian* to deserve the name of Christian, yea, the moderns both *Papists* and *Lutherans*, that wrot against the *Socinians*, deny them also to be Christians, the same doth *Gomarus* and Doctor *Forbes* in his Theological Instructions, *lib.* 10. *cap.* 13. Sect. 14. denyes the *Socinian* Baptism to be valid.

(b) Athanasius *oratione prima contra* Arianos *multis probat* Arianos *non debere dici christianos.*
Idem scribit Theodoretus, *lib.* 2. *cap.* 16. Fulgentius & Hilarius *ad Imperatorem* Constantium.

The Professors of *Leyden, Anno Dom.* 1598. gave their judgment of *Osterodius* the *Socinian* his Writs, that they led Men very near to *Turcism*; and *Grotius* writing of the Piety of the States of *Holland*, saith, *Seing Heresie is the Venom of the Church, and that suddenly working, yet there are degrees in Heresies, whereof some are more hurtful then others, but a worse Heresie then* Socinianism *is not to be found*; at the very mentioning of which all the godly should shrink.

Against this Heresie, not only the Civil Magistrate and Church, but also the God of Heaven by His immediate Hand of Providence hath given Testimony; the Magistrate hath put them to death, not only in the reformed Church, but also the *Roman* Church: Thus the Parliament of *Pole* being informed *Anno Dom.* 1638. that the *Socinians* in *Racovia* had begun to print a Book of Blasphemies against the Sacred Trinity,

Trinity, (a) they did take from them their Bibliotheck, Printing-house, and Press, and being many, banished them the Town: As for the immediate Hand of God upon the *Socinian*, it is remarkable both in Temporal and Spiritual Judgments, that some of them were their own Murderers, and others of them died in Despair, others renounced Christ and turned *Mahumetan*.

    Thus having spoken of the *Socinian*, remains a word of the *Anabaptist* and *Quaker*, who also are Blasphemers of the Trinity; That the *Anabaptists* are such, the Professors of *Leyden* are sufficient Witnesses; (b) As for the *Quakers*, who not only are in *England* and *Ireland*, but even some of them scattered in *Scotland*; It's well known by many of their own printed Pamphlets, and by the Books of others, their mad Pranks, and Blasphemies, and Disputes against the Sacred Trinity; for instance; The *Phanatick History* printed at *London*, Anno Dom. 1660. pag. 54. In a publick Dispute at *Cambridge* they denied the Sacred Trinity, with Blasphemies that I abhor to write; And *Anno Dom.* 1657. a Book printed at *London*, by *John Stalham*, called *the Reviler rebuked*, wherein he refutes *Quaker*, *Richard Fairnworth*, who printed and spread a Pamphlet about that time, wherein he denied the Holy Ghost to be a Person in the Trinity. Therefore as the Universal Church of old did piously and wisely appoint and practise the singing of the Doxology, to confirm the Flock of Christ against the dangerous Blasphemies of *Arius*, and other *Antitrinitarian* Hereticks; so to this day the Universal Church do still continue that practice to guard their Flocks against the Blasphemies of *Anabaptists* and *Quakers*, but especially *Socinians*, who in horrid and hellish Blasphemies outdo the old *Arian*.

(a) *Libri titulus, Tormentum Throno Tritnitatem deturbans.*

(b) *Profess. Leidens. disp. 23. in antithesi Sabellius & Praxias, & hodie libertini, & Anabaptistæ quidam, trinominem Deum statuentes, & personarum realem distinctionem tollentes, modumque tantum patefactionis varium inducentes Patrem incarnatum passumque revera statuunt.*

CHAP.

CHAP. VI.

The lawfulness of Singing the Doxology proven by these Arguments. 1. Because all Christians are baptized in the Name of Father, Son, and Holy Ghost. 2. They believe, or profess their Faith, in Father, Son, and Holy Ghost. 3. They believe Father, Son, and Holy Ghost to be their Creator, Redeemer, and Sanctifier. 4. Their Faith, and Hope of Eternal Glory, is from Father, Son, and Holy Ghost. 5. God, Father, Son, and Holy Ghost, made all things, and especially for His Glory. 6. This Lord of Glory often calls Man's Tongue His Glory. 7. From the practice of the Saints and Angels. 8. From God's Command. 9. The Appointment and Practice of the universal Church. 10. The indivisibility of the worship we give to God one in Essence, and three Persons, illustrate by Fathers and Councils.

IN the former Chapters, I having described the occasion upon which the Universal Church did appoint the singing of the Doxology, to wit, The abounding of Blasphemers against the Trinity, proven in the first three Chapters. Secondly, The unanimous Agreement of the Church for singing the Doxology in the fourth Chapter, and the reason of its continuance in the Church to this day, even because the Church ever since hath never altogether wanted some blasphemous Hereticks within the Church, besides the *Turk* and *Jew*, both deniers of the Trinity without the Church. Follows the second part of this Treatise, which is subdivided thus: First, I prove by many Arguments the lawfulness of the singing of the Doxology, in the sixth, seventh, eighth, ninth, and tenth Chapters: Secondly, I answer some Objections in the eleventh, and twelfth Chapters: Thirdly, I show the many Evils from the refusing to sing the Doxology; Lastly, I close with an Exhortation to receive with all tenderness, all that shall return from their Errors.

In this and some following Chapters, I have accumulate Arguments, because, I supposed I did write to some Christians weak in Knowledge, I say weak in Knowledge, because I am loath to judge that any Christian strong in Knowledge will deny its lawfulness, unless their Judgement be strangely overclouded by prevalent Prejudice, and if any such there be, we have also brought Arguments for their perusing: We begin with Arguments for the Weak.

All who are baptized in the Name of Father, Son, and Holy Ghost, to them it is lawful to sing Glory to Father, Son, and Holy Ghost: But all Christians are baptized in the Name of Father, Son, and Holy Ghost; therefore, to all Christians it's lawful to sing Glory to Father, Son, and Holy Ghost.

The Doxology Approven.

Second Reason, All who believe and profess their Faith in Father, Son, and Holy Ghost, to them it's lawful to sing Glory to Father, Son, and Holy Ghost, but all Christians throughout the World believe and profess Faith in Father, Son, and Holy Ghost, therefore it is lawful to all Christians throughout the World to sing Glory to Father, Son, and Holy Ghost.

Third Reason, All who believe or profess that God, Father, Son, and Holy Ghost, is their Creator, Redeemer, and Sanctifier; to them it is lawful to sing Glory to Father, Son, and Holy Ghost: But all Christians believe and profess, that God, Father, Son, and Holy Ghost, is their Creator, Redeemer, and Sanctifier; Therefore, &c.

Fourth Reason, All who believe, hope, and profess to enjoy eternal Glory in Heaven, from and with Father, Son, and Holy Ghost, to them it is lawful to sing Glory to Father, Son, and Holy Ghost: But all Christians believe, hope, and profess to enjoy eternal Glory in Heaven, from and with the Father, Son, and Holy Ghost; Therefore, &c.

Fifth Reason, God Father, Son, and Holy Ghost, made all things for His own Glory, and Man's chief end is to glorifie God, the first words of the lesser Catechism of the *Westminster* Synod; Therefore it is lawful for Man to glorifie Father, Son, and Holy Ghost, in a Song.

Sixth Reason, God Father, Son, and Holy Ghost hath given to Man his Tongue and Speech, that therewith he may glorifie God Father, Son, and Holy Ghost; Therefore, often in the Book of *Psalms*, Mans Tongue is called his glory, Psal. 57. 8. *Awake up my glory*. Psal. 108. 1. *I will sing praise with my glory*. Psal. 16 9. *My heart is glad, my glory rejoyceth*; which glory, the Maker of the Tongue (Acts 2. 26.) expones to be the Tongue, in these words, *My heart did rejoyce, and my tongue was glad*. Psal. 30. 12. *That my glory may sing praise unto thee, and not be silent, O Lord my God*: Shall then, Mans Tongue, his glory, be commanded silence by Man, and not to sing glory to God the Father, Son, and Holy Ghost, when his Maker gave him his Tongue to sing glory to his Maker.

Seventh Reason, That which is the practice of the Angels, and of all the Saints in Heaven and Earth, is lawful, but to sing glory to God Father, Son, and Holy Ghost, is the practice of the Angels, Luk. 2. 14. *The heavenly host sang glory to God*, and Rev. 5. 13. All in Heaven and in Earth did sing glory to God.

Eighth Reason, That which is commanded of God is lawful, but to sing glory to God is commanded by God, I prove the assumption, Psal. 96. 1, 2. These commanded, *Sing unto the Lord*, and vers. 3. *declare his glory*, and vers. 7, 8. *give unto the Lord the glory due unto his Name*. &c.

Ninth Reason, That which hath been the constitution and constant practice of the Universal Church these 1300. Years without scruple, or refusal, and still retained in all the reformed Churches, after their purgation

purgation from Idolatry and Superstition, that is lawful ; the same Argument is used by St. *Paul*, 1 *Cor.* 11. 16. to stop the mouth of the Contentious, to wit, *we have no such custom, neither the Churches of God.*

Teach Reason, (*a*) That which is commanded by God is lawful; but to sing glory to Father, Son, and Holy Ghost, is commanded by God; Therefore, *&c.* I prove the *minor*, the glory commanded by God, and given to God is indivisive, and due to all the three Persons equally; so says the lesser *Catechism*, they are equal in Power and Glory, and whensoever a Christian sings glory to God, then it is not only lawful, but also necessary that in the thought that Christian at that same time shall ascribe that glory to all the three Persons, which if he do not, he is worshipping an Idol, and not the true God; then, whatever thought of a Christian is lawful and commanded, it is lawful for him to express that thought with his Tongue then when he is singing glory to God, and lawfully and equally in his Mind is giving that glory to Father, Son, and Holy Ghost, then it is lawful for him at that same time to give that glory expresly with his Tongue to Father, Son, and Holy Ghost, for all the Worship and Adoration that the Christian gives to God, should, and is rightly given to God, one in Essence, and three in Persons, Father, Son, and Holy Ghost, who all three have one Almighty Power, one Will, one external Action, in hearing our Prayers, and granting our Requests, and therefore the Worship given to them is Indivisible, therefore *Perkins* saith well, writing on *Matth.* 6. *vers.* 9.

(*a*) *Rationis fundamentum illustratum.* Justinus Martyr, *in expositione fidei sive unam, duas, vel tres personas proferamus, necesse est animo semper possidere* ἀχώριστον τὴν ἕνωσιν *de Patre, Filio, & Spiritu Sancto.*

Athanasius *lib. de communi essentia Patris, Filii, & Spiritus Sancti,* cap. oo. *quod non sunt tres dij* ἀμέριςτ᾽ ἡ ἀξία μια βασιλεια μια δυναμις και βυλη και ενεργεια εδιοξυσα τηυ τριαδα απο της κτισεως ενα λεγω θεου. Idem in Symbolo τριας εν μοναδι και μονας εν τριαδι λατρυεται ὁ θελων συν σωθηναι ετο περι της αγιας τριαδος *pa-gi*170.

Basilius *magnus lib.* 5. *contra* Eunomium *cap.* 15. μη μερισης τα αμερισα, ἡ τριας σεβασμιος εςιν εν μια, και αιδιω: ασχιςως, αδιαιρετως----μηδχιζε τα ασχιςα, καν γαρ θελεις ὁ σχιζεται, *licet hæretici disrumpant sese non tamen disrumpetur Trinitas.*

Nazianzenus *Orat.* 40. *Quæ est in sanctum baptisma* βαπτισω σε μαθητον εις ονομα πατρος, και υιυ, και πνευματ᾽ αγιου, ονομα δε κοινον των τριων. Idem Orat. 37. τυ ἑνος προσκυνησις, των τριων ες προσκυνησις, δια το εν τοις τρισιν ὁμοτιμον της αξιας της θεοτητος.

Ephiphanius *Hæresi* 62. §. 3. μια υσα θευτης, μια κυριοτης, μια δοξολογια υσα.

Hæc eadem est doctrina communiter Scholasticorum Alensis *in summa*

we should worship the whole Trinity conjunctly, and not one Person alone, and when we name God alone, we should in our mind worship the three Persons also; Then upon the sound and infallible Doctrine of Christianity as no Christian dare deny the lawfulness of singing Glory to God, so upon the same ground, and as infalliby, no Christian dare deny the lawfulness of singing Glory to God Father, Son, and Holy Ghost.

Theologiæ parte 3. quest. 3. membro 1. Articulo 3. Aquinas 2.2. *quest. 81. articulo 3. & quest. 84. articulo 1.* Et Franciscus à Sancto Claro *in expositione confessionis Anglicanæ,* Orat. 28. *negat unam personam divinam præcise sumptam esse terminum formalem adorationis latriæ, sed deitatem primario, & personas ut identificantur cum essentia.*

Calvinus *Institut. lib. 1. cap. 13. §. 2. Si non consideramus tres personas in deitate, nudum, & inane duntaxat Dei nomen sine vero Deo in cerebro nostro volitat, & §. 6. ubi in Scripturis sit simplex Dei mentio, & indefinita non minus ad Filium, & Spiritum Sanctum pertinet nomen hoc quam ad patrem. Et §. 20. In eundem sensum* Amesius *medull. lib. 1. c. 6. §. 26. Equalis honor omnibus personis divinis equaliter à nobis debetur.*

The ninth Reason in this Chapter being taken from the Custome of the Church, and that in Imitation of the Apostle *Paul*, 1 *Cor.* 11. *ver.* 16. For in this present Case, the duty being proven lawfull, according to the Word of God, which we have done in the former eight Reasons; the practice of the Church (if the Apostles Argument hold good) is sufficient warrand to clear the Conscience, of every particular Christian, for doing of the duty; therefore, albeit we have handled before somewhat of the Antiquity, and Universality of this Practice, in singing the Doxology, and using it in our Devotion, yet for furder clearing of that truth, and satisfaction to the scrupulous, we shall clear it yet more from Antiquity; St. *Basil*, who was mighty in the Scriptures, and a Son of thunder against the *Arian* in his time, and so took occasion to write of the Doxology, being the great badge, and standard of Christinaity against the *Arian*, writs thus, (*a*) That he received the Custome of singing Glory to the Father, as an Heirship from his Fathers, learned it at him that baptized him, and cites many of the Ancient Fathers, even to the dayes of the Apostles that used the Doxology, and that the Fathers before him did appoint it to be sung in their Kirks, and as this shows it's antiquity, so

(*a*) Basil *tomo 2d. lib. de spiritu sancto, cap. 29. consuetudinem psallendi Doxologiam habemus acceptam ab antiquitate Patrum & proavorum, pag.* 218. *citat non solum* Irenæum, *sed &* Dionysium Alexandrium, *ad* Dionysium Romanum *his verbis scribentem, congruenter nos formâ à Senioribus acceptâ concordibus votis Patri, & filio Domino nostro Jesu Christo, cum Spi-*
he

The Doxology Approven. 43

he writs accordingly of his univerſality, that from the East and the West, Meſopotamia and Cappadocia, Nations, and Cities long before his time, and the memory of all men uſed the Doxology.

But if it be objected, that yet it's uncertain when the Church first began to ſing the Doxology in the publick worſhip of God, and therefore it is to be rejected, I anſwer, *First,* The duty being lawfull, and infallibly grounded on the Word of God, ſo it cannot be denyed, but the uſing of it is very Ancient, in the Church of Chriſt. 2d. Anſwer, by the light of Nature, and Law of Nations, a conſtant good Cuſtome, long practiſed many hundred years without controle, or any apparent evil in the practice thereof, turns into a Law, (*b*) for univerſal practice, anſwers to univeral voices, that all who practiſe it, are content that it be a Law, and as it is ſo in the State, by Analogy, it is ſo in the Church, therefore St. *Paul* does not reaſon from a Church Canon, he ſayes not we have made an Act in the Church for ſuch a thing to be done, but only this, *the Church hath no ſuch cuſtome,* therefore, would he ſay, this is as ſtrong as a Church Act. 1 *Corinth.* 11. 16. I am glad that the Synod of Divines did not reject the Apoſtolick Creed, but has retained it at the end of their Shorter Catechiſm, albeit they cannot tell no more then *Calvin* when it was firſt written, or made uſe of in the Church, but confeſſes it Orthodox, lawfull, and conſonant

tu ſancto ſit gloria, & impertum in ſecula ſeculorum: imo teſtatur Clementem cujus multæ extant Epiſtolæ adeiſque Apoſtolis contemporarium fuiſſe uſum Doxologiâ, & Originem, & Africanum Hiſtoricum, & Gregorium Thaumaturgon, & Firmilanium in ſuis libris, quod ad ſuam praxin lib. de Spiritu Sancto, cap. 7. pag. 157. de ſeipſo ita ſcribit, ὅτι ἐρ ἐλεγον Ἰοι νυν οἱ πατέρες ἡμῶν και ἡμεῖς λεγομεν ὅτι ἡ δοξη κ̅υ̅ν̅ πατρι και υνι δια και μεγα Ιηυννα ἰων δοξολογιαν πρασαγομεν.

(*b*) Baſil *de ſpiritu ſancto. cap.* 27. ειδε τον τροπον Ιης δοξολογιας ὁς αγραφον παρεῖεν]αι δοσαν ἡμιν της τε κατα]νν πιςιν ὁμολογιας]ας αποδειξεις.

Quod ſi glorificandi modum veluti ſcripto non traditum rejiciant proferant nobis fidei profeſſionis probationem de ſcripturis Calvinius inſtitut. lib. 2. *cap.* 16. § 18. *hactenus ſymboli Apoſtolici Orationem ſecutus ſum, quia dum paucis verbis capita redemptionis perſtringit, vice tabulæ nobis eſſe poteſt, in qua diſtincte & ſigillatim reſpicimus, quæ in Chriſto attentione digna ſunt, Apoſtolicum autem nuncupo de authore interim minime ſolicitus, Apoſtolis certè magno ſcriptorum veterum aſſenſu adſcribitur, ſive quod ab illis in commune conſcriptum, ac æditum exiſtimabant, ſive quod compendium iſtud ex doctrina per eorum manus tradita, bona fide collectum, tali elegio confirmandum cenſerunt, neque vero Authori dubium eſt quin à prima ſtatim Eccleſiæ origine adeoque ab ipſis Apoſtolorum ſæculis inſtar, publicè, & omnium calculis receptæ confeſſionis obtinuerit, undicunque tandem*

to

to the Scriptures, and very ancient, and in all these it aggrees with the Doxology, then if you retain your Creed, albeit none tell who first wrote it, or when it was first made use of, so I plead for the Doxology, that same priviledge, that albeit it cannot be proven from Scripture, when it began to be used, yet it having all the good properties of the Creed, should be retained in the Church as long as the Creed.

Yea, seeing the Creed retains the style Apostolick, because of it's great Antiquity, so some of the learned incline to think, that the Doxology is also of Apostolick antiquity, for that it was used in the Church long before the *Nicen* Creed. It was proven by *Basils* words, and *Athanasius*, who was a young Presbyter at the Council of *Nice*, and there a great refuter of *Arius*, yet long before he dyed, *Basil* writs diverse Letters to him, *Epist.* 47. And diverse following reverencing his Gray Hairs, but so as they were Bishops contemporary, and *Bazil* writs, that the D.xology was used in *Europ*, and *Asia* long before the Council of *Nice* even past the memory of Men, and seing in the Primitive Kirk many Catechumine Men and Women were solemnly Baptized in their publick worship, who had chiefly learned in their Catechism the Doctrine of the Trinity, and gave a confession of it at their Baptism themselves, and in that their publick worship were alwayes sung holy Hymnes to God (as the learned know) what more probable then that these, especially the Catechumeni who were now Christians of understanding, as they were Baptized presently in the name of Father, Son, and Holy Ghost, and gave a Confession of their Faith, in Father, Son, and Holy Ghost, that they also in their publick worship did sing Glory, to that Father, Son, and Holy Ghost, In whose name they were newly Baptized.

Some asks the question, upon what Text of Scripture the Doxology is chiefly founded, for answer: It hath two parts, to wit, The three Persons of the Trinity, which are the object of that worship: Secondly, the Glory given to them, which is the Act of worship in the Doxology, accordingly, the giving of Glory to God is founded on many Scriptures, but there is one full, and express, *Rom.* 11. the last *verse, Of him, and through him, and to him are all things, to whom be glory for ever,*

initio fuerit profectum, nec ab uno aliquo privatim fuisse conscriptum vere est quamsimile ab ultima usque memoria sacrosanctæ inter pios omnes authoritatis fuisse constet; quod unice curandum est, id extra omnem contraversiam positum habemus totam in ea fidei nostræ historiam succinctè, distinctoque ordine recenseri, nihil autem contineri quod solidis scripturæ testimonijs non sit consignatum: quo intellecto de authore vel anxie laborare, vel cum alioquo digladiari nihil attinet, nisi qui forte non suficiat certam habere spiritus sancti veritatem, ut non simul intelligat aut cujus ore nunciata, aut cujus manu descripta fuerit.

ever, Amen. But feing the object of the worſhip, in three diſtinct Perſons of the Trinity is moſt clear in the Words of the Baptiſmal inſtitution, *Matth.* laſt, Baptizing them in the Name of the Father, and the Son, and the Holy Ghoſt; therefore with *Athanaſius, Bazil,* and the reſt of the Greek Fathers, we think that the Doxology is chiefly grounded upon that Text in *Matthew.* It is true, ſome of the Learned would build it on that Text, *Rom.* 11. And that becauſe they alleadge the three Perſons of the Trinity Inſinuate here, which though it were granted, that the three Perſons are there inſinuat, yet the other Text being full and expreſs, and the ſtrongeſt Bulwark againſt the *Arian,* therefore that Text in *Matthew,* is the chief ground for the Doxology, for to glorify God according to that Text in the *Romans* is ſo general, that the *Arian* could eaſily ſubſcribe to ſuch a Doxology.

Lombardus lib. 1. ſenten. diſtinct. 36. capitulo 3. putat cum Auguſtino in lib. 1. de trinitate, cap. 6 in loco prædicto 11. capitis ad Romanos indigitari diſtinctionem trium perſonarum: aſtibi certum eſt eo loco non ſatis perſpicuum datur fundamentum fidei trium perſonarum trinitatis, & pro argumento invincibili quod Eunomius Arianus iſtam textam citat, ut patet Baſilei, lib. 1. contra Eunominium dum dat confeſſionem ſuæ fidei, pag. 7. Credimus inquit, in unum Deum, ex quo ſunt omnia, & in unum unigenitum dei filium eundem verbum dominum noſtrum Jeſum Chriſtum per quam ſunt omnia, & in unum Spiritum Sanctum paracletum. Hæc Arij confeſſio fidei in trinitatem ſubolet hunc locum ad Romanos & ipſe Arianus prius rumperet quam confiteretur ſe credere in Patrem Filium & Spiritum Sanctum aut ita proferret Doxologiam, ut ſcribit Baſilius.

CHAP. VII.

The lawfulneſs of ſinging the Doxology, proven by the Induction of all it's Parts 12. *from the three Holies,* Iſa. 6. 3.

IN this Chapter we prove by Induction, that all the Parts of the Doxology are in the Holy Scriptures, from whence we deduce this Reaſon; that Divine Glory which in the Holy Scripture is given to Father, Son, and Holy Ghoſt, that ſame Divine Glory is lawfull to ſing to Father, Son, and Holy Ghoſt; we prove the aſſumption, that Glory is given to Father, Son, and Holy Ghoſt, *Rom.* 11. *v.* laſt, *To God be glory for ever,* 1 Tim: 1. 17. *To God be honour and glory forſor ever and ever, Amen.* 2 Tim. 4. 18. *To God be glory for ever and ever,* 1 Tim. 6. *v.* 16. *To God be honour and power everlaſting for ever,* Jude *v.* laſt, *To God be glory now and for ever, Amen.* Galat. 14. 5.

To God and our Father be glory for ever and ever, Amen. and the same Words Philip. 4. 20. Secondly, *Glory to God through Christ*, these words you shall find, *Rom.* 16. v. last. *Eph.* 3. 21. *Heb.* 13. 20, 21.

Thirdly, *To Christ be glory now and for ever, Amen.* 2 Peter 3. v. last, Revel. 16. Revel. 5. 12. *He is the Lord of glory,* 1 Corinth. 2. 8. James 2. 1. *He is crowned with glory,* Heb. 2. 9. *The Lords glorious branch* Isaiah, 11. 10.

The Holy Ghost, Pet. 14. 14. *The Spirit of glory is glorified.*

Thus we have proven from Scripture these parts of the Doxology, Glory to the Father, to the Son, and Holy Ghost, for now and ever: There remains one word to be cleared in the Doxology, to wit, *As it was in the beginning*, for clearing of which, we wrot in the end of the fourth Chapter, that these words were added to the Doxology, because of *Arian Hereticks*, and that in the fourth Century, when *Arius* denyed that the Son was with the Father from all eternity, but affirmed that there was a time when the Son was not, and these Ancient Doctors of the Church, knowing that the first Words in St. *Johns* Gospel, in these three Verses, were indited by the Holy Ghost, and written by the Apostle *John* his Pen-man, to assert the Co-eternity of the Son with the Father, and that against Ancient Hereticks, who lived in the Apostle St. *John's* time, and were Blasphemers of Christ, the Church therefore hath made choise of that same Text, as fittest against the *Arians* (a) Thus have we cleared, that all the Words in the Doxology, are express Scripture, and according thereunto; and if any object, that it follows not to be lawfully sung in the Church, except it were in Scripture, all contiguous together as one of the *Psalms* of *David*, to these in this place, I only give this Answer, That the reformed Church of *France*, in their publick worship sing the Apostolick Creed turned in Meeter, and is therefore printed, and bound in with their *Psalm* Books, and yet that Creed is far lesse continued Scripture then the Doxology. And the Learned know, that the Church of *France* is famous not only of old time, for many glorious Martyres before the Council of *Nice*, but also in the beginning of Reformation from Popery.

(a) *Alexander Alexandriæ Episcopus Concilij Niceni Membrum Arij Blasphemiis insensissimus, in sua Epistola ad omnes ubique gentium fratres scribit Arium asserere tempus aliquando fuisse cum filius Dei non esset, quod sic refutat in initio Evangilij Joannis. In principio erat verbum, itaque non erat tempus cum non esset Socrates lib. 1. cap. 3. & Syrmiense concilium in symbolo damnat eos qui dicunt, erat tempus, aut seculum quando λόγος non erat: ibidem anathemate 2ç. Si quis dicat Christum ex quo, ex Maria natus est initium accepisse, ut Deus esset anathema sit, ut* Samosatenus, Ebion, & Cerinthus.

The

The Doxology Approven. 47

(a) The second Part of the Chapter containing the twelfth Reason, it is taken from *Isaiah cap.* 6. *v.* 1, 2. 3. The Prophet *Isaiah* in a vision saw the Lord sitting on a Throne, and the heavenly seraphims crying one to another *holy, holy, holy is the Lord of hosts, the whole earth is full of his glory.* Here the learned prove, that this song is sung to the Sacred Trinity, as if these Seraphims had said, Holy Father, Holy Son, Holy Ghost; for that same Lord of Hosts, in the 8. *v.* speaks in the plural number *who will go for us*, just so, *Gen.* 1. 26. *And God said let us make man after our likeness*: which speech the learned agree to be spoken by the Sacred Trinity. Secondly, We shall prove that glory to the three distinct Persons of the Trinity is meant here, *First*, That glory to the Father is meant none will deny, no not the *Arian*, nor *Socinian*. Secondly, we prove that glory to the Son is also meant here, for God the Son was also here, for the Prophet *Isaiah* saw his glory here, which is proven, *John* 12. 41. The Prophet *Isaiah* saw Christs glory, and spake of Him even then, when the Lord blinded their eyes, and hardened their hearts, *Verse* 40. which commission *Isaiah* received, *Isaiah* 6. 10. after he had seen Christs glory, then if God the Son was here, the 2d, holy is to him. *Thirdly*, the Holy Ghost was here, which I prove, it was the Holy Ghost here which spake to the Prophet *Isai.* 6. 9. *The Lord said, go tell this people;* but *Acts* 28. 25. That same

(b) Origines, *in hunc locum*, II. 66. 3. *ait hic trinitatem insinuari* Athanasius, *tom.* 1. *operim pag.* 154. 255. προσφέρει την δοξολογίαν αγιος αγιος αγιος λεγοντα τως τρεις υποςάσεις τηλείας δεικνύντα εςιν ως και εν τω λέγειν κύριος την μίαν ουσίαν δηλοσιν. proferunt. glorificationem, *dicentes sanctus, sanctus, sanctus, tres personas perfectas ostendunt, & sub una voce Dominus unam substantiam declarant idque* ασυγχύτως και αμίκτως, *in confuse, & indivise sub-innuens, nec Angelos nec Homines debere nec audere colere essentiam divinam, & non una colere tres personas ut supra probatum, hoc idem* Athanasius *ait detestandos ac procul abigendos esse* Arianos *dicentes ac si ipsi interfuissent angelos illos in primis vocibus exclamandi sanctus maxima voce usos esse, in secundis autem non tam magna voce, in tertia, adhuc submissiori, ac primam sanctificationem propriam legitimamque esse, secundam autem inferioris notae, tertiam adhuc gradatim deterioris conditionis esse: In eandem sententiam scribit* Caesarius Gregorij Nazianxeni *frater dialogo primo responsione ad interrogationem* 13. Epiphanius *in ancorato* § 10. & 26. τριάδα δοξάζοντες ουν εν ενοτητε και ενοτητα εν τριάδι *hic hymnus* Isaiah. 6. 3. *quem* Gre. το τρισάγιον *vocant canitur in liturgiis* Basil, Chrisostom. & Gregorij, *ut* Damascenus, *lib.* 3. Orthodoxæ fidei, *cap.* 10. *interpretatur quod ter sanctus, sit tribus personis trinitatis* τρισαγιος. αγιωσιαν; *in ordine baptismi secundum* Æthiopes *habetur* Sanctus, Sanctus, Sanctus Pater, Filius & Spiritus Sanctus,

Lord is the Holy Ghost; well spake the Holy Ghost by *Isaiah* the Prophet unto our Fathers, saying, *Go unto this people and say, hearing ye shall hear, and shal not understand,* &c. Then seing the Scriptures prove the three Persons expresly were here, it cannot be denyed, but the three holies were to the three Persons; therefore the Doctors of the Ancient Church, and universal Councills, and approven Orthodox Divines, unanimously teach, that here the *Seraphims* in their Chore are singing a Doxology to the blessed Trinity, and consequently this Doxology is a Scripture Song, therefore the Divines of *Westminster* Synod, in their Notes upon *Revel.* 4. at the 8. *Verse* singing the like three Holies with them, in the 6. of *Isaiah* 3. *Verse*, which they also quoat, and coment thus; They contiually praise God, and set out the Trinity of the Persons in the Godhead.

Did not the Angels, in this 6. of *Isaiah* sing the Doxology to the Glorious Trinity? The universall Church in their General Councill have taught so, and also practised accordingly, The Fathers, both before, and after that Councill, with *Calvine*, and the rest of the

nunc & semper, & in secula seculorum Amen. Anno Dom. 451. *Hic hymnus trisagius in Concil œcumen. Chaledon.* 630. *Episcoporum fuit cantatus, & inter acta hujus Concilij refertur; & postea Ecclesia universalis eo hymno est usa, ut colligitur ex* Constantinopolitana *Sinodo.* 5. *Præsidente* Menua *ejus sedis Patriarcha, ubi* Petrus Gnapheus Antiochiæ *Episcopus damnatus quod in suæ Ecclesiæ* Lyturgia He*retice trisagio,* Sanctus, Sanctus, Sanctus *addidisset qui pro nobis crucifixus est, ubi per ter sanctus interpretantur, tres Personas Trinitatis, ut videre est in Epistola monitoria ad eundem* Gnapheum, *prioribus consentiunt* Theodoretus *sermone,* 2do. *de curandis Grec. affecto.* Cyrillus *in eum textum,* Augustinus *sermone* 38 *de tempore, Et hæc eadem est sententia theologorum, modernorum* Calvini *institut, lib.* 1. *cap.* 13. Is. 6. *cap.* § 11. & 15. & 28. Zanchij *tomo.* 1. *lib.* 1. *cap.* 2. Isa. 6. *cap.* Seraphim *occinunt Patri Filio & Spiritui* Sancto, *quod etiamsi* Antitrinitarij *Transilvanij negent, hunc textum nunquam mihi eripient.* Polani *syntagmate lib.* 9. *cap.* 15. *Professores* Leidenses *disp.* 7. *thesi* 16. Bucan. *loco* 3. § 7. Ames. *medull. lib.* 1. *cap.* 5 § 17.

reformed Church teached so, and the Synod of Divines in their Notes on the *Revelation* teached so; will ye not then go along with the Universall, and Reformed Church, or will ye go along with the Synod of Divines on the *Revelation*; to that Synod you gave the Credit to draw up your Creed, or Confession of Faith, and Catechisms, and will ye not give them credit in the matter of the Doxology, that the Heavenly Seraphims sang Glory to Father, Son, and Holy Ghost, shall the Angels come from Heaven to Earth, to give you a good example to sing the Doxology; will neither the Universal
Church

Church on Earth, nor Angels in Heaven move you to follow their holy example, I answer, It will move all these on whom that Judgement hath not fallen, pronouuced, *Isaiah* 6. 9, 10. *Hear indeed, but understand not, make the heart of this people fat*: As ye love your Souls, bewar of that Judgement, which is my prayer for you at the Throne of Grace.

CHAP VIII.

13. *Reason from that Song*, Revel. 5. 9. 14. *From Gods Command*, 1 Chr. 16. 20. *Illustrat by Councils and Fathers.*

THe thirteenth reason is taken from the 5. Chap. of the Book of *Revelation*, thus collected; *John* the Divine saw a vision in Heaven, and heard them sing a new Song, *vers.* 9. continuing to the end of the Chapter: and *vers.* 13. *Every creature which is in heaven, and on the earth, and under the earth, and such as are in the sea, and all that are in them, heard I saying, blessing, honour, glory, and power be unto him that sitth upon the Throne, and unto the Lamb for ever and ever.* Here the th:rsity of singing is so great, that it comprehends the universal ar:rch of all Christians, yea, of all the Angels in Heaven, and all Saints Heaven and Earth, both the Church Militant, and Triumphant. What are they singing? *Blessing, honour, glory, and power.* 3. To whom do they sing this *Doxologie*? I answer, *to him that sits upon the Throne, and to the Lamb*: And that the weak may better understand that there are two Persons of the Godhead distinctly exprest here, for them more clearly distinguished in the 6. *vers. In the midst of the Throne stood a Lamb, who came and took the Book out of the right hand of him that sat upon the Throne*, *Verf.* 7. And that both the Father and the Son sat upon the same Throne, *Revel.* 3. 21. at the end, *I am set down with my Father on his Throne.* And *Revel.* 22. 3. and 1. *verses*, both *the Throne of God and of the Lamb*, and not Thrones. But the weak may say that the Holy Ghost is not named in this Song? To whom I answer, that it is the Doctrine and Faith of the universal Church, containing all Christians, from the rising of the Sun to its going down, Father, Son, and Holy Ghost, one and that same glorious God sit and reign conjunctly upon one and that same glorious Throne in Heaven, according to the lesser Catechism, *There are three Persons in the Godhead, equal in power and*

Athanasius lib. 1. *de Communi essentia trium personarum probat Trinitatem sedere in Throno*, Nazianzenus *Orat.* 26. *Docet Spiritum Sanctum esse Patre Filioque*, σуμφυες και ὁμοδοξον και ὁμοτιμον και συνθρονον, & *in Lyturgia Graco Tomo* 2. *Bibliotheca Patrum*

glory;

glory: So that here while they sing glory to him that sits upon the Throne, the Holy Ghost is also necessarily to be meant, and lawfully is to be expressed, according to the orthodox Doctrine in the former reasons. *Græc. Latin. pag.* 112. *Ita Deum invocant, ἄναρχε τριάς ἀμέρις ἐστία σύνθρονε μονάς, expers principii Trinitas impartibilis essentia eidem incidens throno unitas.* Seing then all the Saints and Angels in Heaven and in Earth joyn in this Song with a loud voice, what a pity is it that some Christians should refuse to joyn in singing this Doxologie, yea, abhor it as a sinful action, and by shuning it, think they abstain from evil? I beseech you in the fear of the Almighty consider that word, *Isai.* 5. 20. *Wo unto them that call evil good, and good evil.*

The General Assembly of this Church, *Anno Dom.* 1647. at *Edinburgh, August* 28. *Sess.* 25. did ordain Mr. *Zacharie Boyd* to turn the Scriptural Songs (beside the Psalms) in the Old and New Testament in Meeter, for the use of the Church, as Mr. *Zacharie* himself professes in the Preface to the said Songs, Printed at *Glasgow, Anno Dom.* 1648. But this Song in the *Revelation* 5. 9. I find not among the Scriptural Songs; why he omitted it, the reason I know not, but this I know, the Holy Ghost calls it a Song as expresly as any in the Bible. 2. The singers are all Christians. 3. The Subject is solemn, and this duty undenyable to all that call themselves Christians. Mr. *Zacharie Boyd* in his Letter to the Ministers of *Scotland*, of the date, *Glasgow*, 27. of *February*, 1648. (which Letter he prefixes to his Scriptural Songs which he turned in Meeter) sayes that the Church having the use thereof, may in obedience to the Apostles Precept, *Eph.* 5. 18. *In Psalms, and Hymns, and spiritual Songs, make melodie in their heart to the Lord.*

The 14th reason that we bring, is from 1 *Chron.* 16. 29. *Give unto the Lord the glory due unto his Name*; whence with a little Explication the lawfulness of singing the Doxologie may be proven: And first, from Christs words in his Divine Institution of Baptism, *Mat.* 28. *verf.* 19. *Baptize all Nations in the Name of the Father, and the Son, and the Holy Ghost*: So according to Christs words, Father, Son, and Holy Ghost is the Name of God; then seeing we are commanded to give glory to Gods name then to give glory to God the Father, Son, and Holy Ghost. And if any would foolishly cavil here are three names, let this suffice to stop their mouth, that God who is truth it self hath called it, *in the Name*, in the Singular Number, and not *Names*, in the Plural: (*a*) Therefore the Doctors both of the Greek and Latine Church have piously and learnedly dived into the mysterious

(*a*) Justin. *in expositione fidei ἐν τῇ τε βαπτίσματος διδαχῇ συνημμένως ἡμῖν τε πατρός και υἱέ και τε ἁγίε πνεύματος*

cause

cause of this *one Name*, and with one consent they agree that it is to teach the unity of the Essence, together with the Trinity of the Persons, then for our purpose, If Father, Son, and Holy Ghost be the Name of God, and three distinct Persons in the Godhead are to be known and believed necessarily to salvation by all Christians who are baptized in that Name; and seeing God in his mercy and goodness hath made Baptism a Seal, applying to Christians benefits of unspeakable value, given by Father, Son, and Holy Ghost, shall it not then be Gods due from man, and mans duty to God, to give God the glory due unto his Name, even to this his Name, Father, Son, and Holy Ghost, yea, and to sing it; for proof of which, amongst many Texts take the 23. Verse of the foresaid Chapter, 1 *Chron.* 16. *Sing unto the Lord all the earth*. So that from these three Texts, 1 *Chron.* 16. 23. and 29. with *Mat.* 28. and 19 I collect this conclusion, all baptized in the Name of the Father, Son, and Holy Ghost, should sing *Glory to the Father, Son, and Holy Ghost*: and if any object that 1 *Chron.* 16. 29. by Gods name is meant himself, I answer, be it so, but God himself is Father, Son, and Holy Ghost.

ὄνομα παραδίδοται, *In doctrina baptismatis unite nobis Patris & Filii, & Spiritus Sancti, unum nomen traditum est* Athanasius, *lib.* 1. *de unita Deitate Trinitatis, ad* Theophilum *in eundem sensum &* Gregorius, Nazianzenus *Oratione* 40. *quæ est in sanctum baptisma*, ὄνομα ἕκοινον των τριῶις ἐν ἡ θεότης, Epiphanius *hæresi* 62. § 4. ἐν ἑνὶ ὀνόματι τριὰς καλευμένη ἐλ ἐγχειρίον ἀρείου, *in uno nomine Trinitas appellata* Arium *refellit idem in* Ancorato, § 22. τριὰς ἑνὶ ἐν ὀνόματι ἀριθμευμένη Trinitas *in uno nomine nominata* Gaudentius *sermone* 14. *non ait in baptismi institutione in nominibus sed in nomine quia unum Trinitatis est nomen*, & Ambrosius, *lib.* 1. *de Spiritu Sancto, cap.* 14. *in baptismo unum nomen quia unus est Deus*, Augustinus *lib.* 3. *contra* Maximinianum, *cap.* 22. *unum nomen quia hi tres sunt unum*. Fulgentius *ad* Felicem notarium, *cap.* 2. *nomen unum Deitatis quod triplicari non potest idem observant*. Lombardus & Aquinas.

Now Christian, when you have read these reasons, I intreat you to lay them to heart, especially the first nine, being most plain, and ponder in each reason the first two sentences, which no Christian will or dare deny, albeit he know no more but the common grounds of reason, and Christianity: and if you grant both the first sentences, and yet deny the third sentence following on that reason, then know that truth hath got the victory, and you are convinced: And if you assent not to sing the Doxologie, ye *detain the truth in unrighteousness*, Rom. 1: 18. and rebel against the light, and hate the light, *John* 3. 20. And they who wilfully harden themselves, would not embrace the truth, albeit Christ the wisdom of the Father were Preaching it unto them, unlesse

he

he did apply his Almighty gracious power, as he did to *Saul* in his conversion, *Acts* 9. ver. 5, 6. Which he does not ordinarily on those that harden themselves, and close their eyes against the light, darting in upon their understanding; for *he resists the proud, but giveth grace to the humble* and lowly. The Apostle speaks of unreasonable men, by which are meant the unbeliever, and unregenerat; For the true believer his saving Faith clears up, and fortifies his reason: Therefore if thou be a furnished and true believer, and grant the truth of the first two sentences of any one, or all the reasons, then thou will assent to the third sentence, which is, to sing *Glory to the Father, Son, and Holy Ghost*; and if thou find thy heart inclining to consent, then blow at that spunk that is kindled in thy soul by the Holy Ghost, and go to thy knees in all humility, sincerity, and self-denial, and beg of him to lead thee in all truth, and to shew thee the good and the right way, and whether it will tend more to the glory of God, to sing *Glory to the Father, Son, and Holy Ghost*, or to be dumb and silent, and say in your heart, I will not sing glory to God, even when my fellow-Christians are singing it.

Do you believe with all your soul that God sent his Son from Heaven to earth to bring you from earth to Heaven; that Christ suffered the sorrows of death and hell, to save thee from endless torments, and will ye refuse to sing glory to him for so doing and suffering for you; If a poor brother of Jesus were asking an alms from you, and you would not give him one mite, and yet would say at that same time to standers by, if that poor man were going to Prison, I would give him a great sum of money to relieve him, would they believe you, or rather laugh you to scorn? So when you are desired to sing glory to the blessed Trinity, and ye refuse to do it, who would believe you that you would suffer tormenting flames for the glory of that blessed Trinity. I know you will say you have some reasons why you refuse to sing the Doxologie, but ye would have no reason to refuse martyrdome? I answer, your corruption, that prompts you with excuses to refuse to sing the Doxologie, which is the easier duty, would furnish you with more excuses to shun burning; so that ye who will not give God his due honour, to sing glory to him, it is too like would never suffer martyrdome for him, and so the true ground of your refusing is want of true Faith, *Phil.* 1. 29. *To you it is given in the behalf of Christ, not only to believe in him, but also to suffer for his sake.*

As for your pretences and excuses you bring for not singing the Doxologie, lay it to heart, that your excuses which your prejudged Conscience it may be accepts of, so as to give you a seeming and deceitful peace for a time; yet trust not that he who is greater then your Conscience will accept of these excuses, which in this life men who are blind, and partial Judges in their own cause thinks to be good

Our Saviour in the Gospel gives a lift of excusers
the Judge of quick and dead tells the true reason
would not have told, *Mat.* 22. 5. *they made light*
t you make it not a light thing to refuse to sing Glo-
and Holy Ghost; for these reasons I have set be-
ed on the Word of God, by which we shall be judg-
:nces and excuses in that day will be burnt with the
Cor. 3. 12.

CHAP. IX.

*e necessary Difference of the Christians Worship, as in
ord, Prayer, and Sacraments, they exceedingly differ
shall not then also be a difference betwixt the Christian
s, and the* Jews : *by singing the* Doxology. 16. *As
Psalms of* David, *close many of them with a* Doxology,
measure of their Light dispensed to them in the Old
recomes the Christian to have a* Doxology *answerable to
sure of Light of the Trinity in the New Testament.* 17.
upon the signification of Jehovah Elohim, *which is of-
logy of the Old Testament.*

asons more to be pondered by the judicious and un-
stian, The first is thus grounded, the Worship of
o parts, either God speaks to us, or we speak to
to us in the Word, read, or exponed by Preaching;
by Prayer, suiting things needful to Soul and Body,
s infinite Excellencies, and for His Benefites. These
Petitions or Praises, are either done without Song or
it is, that God in His infinite Wisdom and Goodness
·istian Worship in the New Testament to differ from
p in the Old Testament, in fulness, clearness, and
they had only the Old Testament, we have the New
o it; they had the Old Testament read and exponed
n and Prophets, we have Old and New Testament
:d and preached more plainly and fully to our greater
and Comfort, *for the least in the kingdom of Heaven*
in Baptist, *Matth.* 11. 11. Secondly, Our Prayers
od in the New Testament are proportional to the
eached, even more full, clear and comfortable then
e Old Testament; but so it is that the obstinate and
fused to joyn with us Christians in any of these three
hip of God; they will not hear the Gospel read, because

cause it is the Gospel of Christ, whom they reject and
will not hear the Word preached, because *we prea(*
which is to the Jews *a stumbling-block*, 1 Cor. 1. 23.
will not joyn with us in Prayer, for they refuse to pr
and Holy Ghost, and they will seek nothing from G
of Christ. Fourthly, They reject our Sacraments,
be baptized in the Name of Father, Son, and Holy G
they communicate with us, because it is the Comm
and Blood of Christ : Seing then the all-wise Lor
Christian to differ from and excell the *Jew* in the
ments, in Preaching and Praying, is it not convenie
the other parts of our Christian Worship, that we d
our singing also, which is not a divers part of Wor
Prayer and Praises without Song, but a divers mann
it ; for example, all that is in the *Psalms*, that is su
Tone ; it is lawful for a Christian to worship Go(
words without a Tone or Song, in Prayer and Than
differ not upon the matter, but in the manner of p
But the adding of the Christian Doxology to the clo
the *Psalm*, makes a suitable difference betwixt the C
the *Psalm* with the Doxology, and the *Jew* in their V
same *Psalm* without the singing of the Christian D
over, Is it convenient or decent, that a *Jew* who bl
of God, and denies the blessed Trinity, who are wit
nion of Saints, that they shall have it to say or brag,
joyn with the Sow, (for so they call the Christian,) n
Gospel read or preached, nor will I joyn with the
they abhor the Name of Christ ;) yet says the *Jew*,
to joyn with them in singing the *Psalm*, for they sir
Psalms of *David* just as we do, they sing in their Mo
do in the *Hebrew*? would not the Christian think
the *Jews* offer, and if any in the Church refused to
he could say I am free to refuse the Doxology as s(
stians refuse.

2. Many of the Psalms close with a Doxology or P
one way some another, and this Doxology is most
Verse ; but sometimes in the *penult* Verse, and ther
some particular reason and ground given for that pa
These who please to search the *Psalms* more dilige
to wit, *Psal.* 18. and 75. in their last and *penult* Vers
Psalms following you may observe a particular D
Verse of every one of them, to wit, *Psalm* 7, 8, 13
41, 45, 52, 57, 59, 61, 66, 68, 71, 72, 89, 97, 99,
124, 136, 140, 145. and besides, there are other

The Doxology Approven. 55

with one and the same Doxology, to wit, *Praise ye the Lord.* Psalm 104, 105, 106, 115, 116, 117, 135, 146, 147, 148, 149, 150. *Hallelujah*, and in the Book of the *Revelation*, chap. 19. three Companies end their Praises to God with that same *Hallelujah*, retaining the *Hebrew* in the *Greek* Text. The first Company much People, verse 1, 2, 3. close their Praises with *Hallelujah*. Secondly, The twenty four Elders, and four living Creatures, in the second Chore, close *Amen, Hallelujah*. Thirdly, Another great multitude, verse 6. being commanded, give their *Hallelujah*.

And as many of the *Psalms* close with a Doxology, so some of the scriptural Songs, as *Exodus* 15. 18. *Isaiah* 12. 6. *Isaiah* 38. 20. *Habakkuk* 3. 18, and 19. 1 *Chronicles* 16. 36: Now, as in the Old Testament the Lord had teached the *Jews* to close their Songs and Psalms with a Doxology, (for in them I find a Doxology about fourty eight times,) so in the New Testament, seing it hath pleased God to reveal Himself more fully then He was pleased to do in the Old Testament to the *Jews*, and make the Doctrine of the Trinity the badge of Christian Baptism, and that Doctrine being so much opposed and blasphemed by *Jews, Turks* and *Hereticks*; shall it not then be lawful and expedient for the Christian, now the only Church of God, to close their Psalms with such a Doxology as may not only be a confession of their Faith in that great fundamental of the Trinity, and foundation of Christianity, but also to discern the true Christian Church from the *Jews* Synagogue, who are now *Lo-ammi* and *Lo-ruhamah*, Hos. 1. 6, 9. and so distinguish them from all other Meetings who pretend to worship the true God, and are but Antichristian Synagogues of Satan, and Blasphemers of the glorious Trinity.

The last Reason may be thus grounded, Amongst the ten several Names whereby God (in the Old Testament) hath been pleased to design Himself, *Jehovah Elohim* are the two chief : First, *Jehovah* is Gods most proper Name, most often used in the Old Testament, it comes from an *Hebrew* word that signifies *To Be*, and so *Jehovah* signifies Gods Essence and Being of Himself, and the giving of Being to all His Creatures ; therefore *Exod.* 6. 3. the Lord prefers His Name *Jehovah* to His other Name *God Almighty*, for this Name implyes Gods Almighty Power, to wit, *Elshaddai*, but *Jehovah* importeth Gods Infinite Perfections ;

יְהוָֹה *Est Dei nomen proprium, & κυριόϊαϊον (cujus contractum* יָהּ *Psal.* 68. 4.) *nunquam legitur cum affixo ante vel post se, ita ut ultima litera nunquam mutetur, est* à radice יָהָה *quod idem cum* הָיָה *fuit est erit & ita Spiritus Sanctus interpretatur, Apocal. cap.* 1. *verf.* 8, ὁ ὢν ϰ ὁ ὢν ϰ ἐρχόμενος λέγει ὁ κύριος ὁ Θεός *significat Dei esse, & existentiam Deo essentialem, adeoque æternam, & omnis entis creati causa*

therefore

therefore *Pſal.* 83. 18. God alone His Name is *Jehovah,* and *Iſa.* 42. 8. I am *Jehovah,* that is my Name, and *Exod.* 15. 3. *Jehovah* is His Name, therefore *Num.* 6. 24, 25, 26. when God endites the words of the Bleſſing to *Moſes,* how the Prieſt ſhould pray over his People, it is all in the Name of *Jehovah,* and ſo the Lord puts His Name *Jehovah* upon His People.

The ſecond Name of God moſt frequent in the Old Teſtament, is *Elohim* ; it is the Plural Number, and is ſometimes indeed uſed in the Old Teſtament in the Singular Number, but not ſo often by far as it's in the Plural Number: It is diſpute among Divines what can be the reaſons why the Lord ſhould take to Himſelf ſo often a Name ſignifying Moe, to wit, a Plurality, and to joyn that to another of His Names, to wit, *Jehovah,* which is of the Singular Number, for albeit often in the Old Teſtament God deſign Himſelf by other moe Names, as *God Almighty, Lord of Hoſts, God of Iſrael,* &c. yet moſt often He deſigns Himſelf *Jehovah Elohim,* which is ordinarily rendered in the Bible, *Lord God* ? For anſwer to the queſtion propoſed, generally it is this, That albeit from theſe two words there cannot be demonſtrate the Unity of the Godhead, and Trinity of the Perſons by a convincing Argument againſt obſtinate *Jews* and *Antitrinitarian* Hereticks, yet from it may be brought a probable Argument to moderate and ſober ſpirited Chriſtians, to prove that *Moſes,* and other Pen-men of the *ſativam, ineſſe, & conſervari, & ita communiter exponunt Theologi, & Rabbini, eſt & tertium Dei nomen ab eadem radice,* Exod. 3. 14. *inquit* Moſes *ſi dicant Egyptij mihi quod nomen ejus Dei qui miſit te ad nos reſpondet Deus* אהיה

אשר אהיה, *quod Arius montanus interpretatur ero quod ero, quod Deus contraxit in immediate ſequentibus* אהיה *miſit me ad vos ERO, quod communiter interpretantur SUM, & in noviſſima Verſione Vernacula* I Am *hæc tria Dei nomina, eandem Dei eſſentiam & exiſtentiam ſignificant, alia duo rarius uſitata, ſed* Jehovah *ſæpiſſime, quod habet nonnunquam alia Dei nomina ſibi adjuncta ut* אדני *adonai,* Judic. *cap.* 16. *v.* 8. *vel* צבאות 1 Sam. *cap.* 1. *verſ.* 11. *&* עליון Pſal. 7. *verſ. ult. ſed ſæpiſſime omnium aſociantur duo nomina* Jehovah Elohim, *verbi gratia, initio verborum Decalogi, Ego* Jehovah Elohim, *hinc in quibuſdam* Pſalmis, *ac aliis Hymnis in Verbo Dei non raro eſt legere* Jehovah Elohim *itaque Doxologiam quaſi* Pſalmi *clauſulam adjungere, ad inſinuandam ſanctiſſimæ Trinitatis glorificationem, ver. gra.* Pſalm 144. *verſ. ult. beatitudines populi cujus* Jehovah אלהיו *in his Doxologiis tres ſunt notabiliores (prima circa initium regni* Dividis *primo libro* Chronicorum *cap.* 16. *verſ.* 35. *ubi* Pſalmum *in publico cetu claudit Doxologia benedictus* Jehovah Elohim *à ſeculo uſque in ſeculum tum dixerunt totus populus,* Amen. 2. Doxologia Jehovah Elohim *eſt*

The Doxology Approven.

Old Testament, who themselves undoubtedly did know the Mystery of the Trinity, as *Moses, David, Isaiah*, &c. and therefore when they did so often write these two Names of God together *Jehovah Elohim*, the first being the Singular Number, the second the Plural, did thereby intimate the Unity of the Essence in the Godhead with the Trinity of Persons; therefore *Pareus* on *Genesis*, pag. 23. having dispute the question, at length concludes, *No godly Man will deny the probability of this reason drawen from* Elohim, *joined with another word of the Singular Number as it is here with* Jehovah; and so think the *Westminster* Synod Notes, on the first two words of *Genesis*, Elohim Bara, the first Elohim being in the Plural Number joyned with Bara in the Singular Number, *He did creat*; and that *Moses*, and the rest of the Pen-men of the Holy Scriptures in the Old Testament did know this Mystery, is out of question to the Doctors, both of the Reformed and *Roman* Church, all which,

primo libro Chron. *cap.* 29. *ubi convocatis regni ordinibus, qui cum* Davide *aurum argentum,* &c. *In Templi structuram liberaliter obtulerunt, tum* David *benedixit publice* Jehovah Elohim, *vers.* 11, *&c. deinde* vers. 20. *edixit* David *toti congregationi benedicite nunc* Jehovah Elohim *sic benedixerunt tota congregatio* Jehovah Elohim, *hæc quidem* Davidis, *& congregationis benedictio videtur absque cantu Deo oblata.* 3. Davidis *Doxologia solemnior* Jehovah Elohim *videtur prorsus ultima jam moribundi inquit* Tremellius *sanctam ipsius animam Deo reddentis,* Psal. 72. 18, 19. *benedictus sit* Jehovah Elohim, *v.* 19. *& benedictum nomen gloriæ ejus in seculum, impleaturque gloriâ ejus tota terra,* Amen *&* Amen. *huic* Davidis *Doxologiæ seraphim,* Isai. *cap.* 6. *vers.* 3. *stantes clamabant Trinitati Doxologiam ut supra probatum est hujus tractatus paginâ* 47. *plena est omnes terra gloriæ ejus; quod quam belle respondet & quasi implet verba* Davidis *nempe impleaturque gloria ejus tota terra.*

with the Fathers and Councils, bring many strong and clear Arguments from the Old Testament to prove the Mystery of the Sacred Trinity: Therefore *Tremellius,* a Jew born, in his Notes upon *Gen.* 1. 26. *Let us make Man after our own image,* saith God; Note this here, God Father, Son, and Holy Ghost, one God in three distinct Persons so appoint; *Let us,* here saith *Tremellius* is a Testimony of the Sacred Trinity, and that not an obscure one: And therefore the *Westminster* Notes prove from the Scriptures, that *Moses* was not ignorant of the Doctrine of the Trinity; and it is observable, that in the first three Chapters of *Genesis, Moses* nineteen times calls God *Jehovah Elohim*; and who will deny that *Abraham* saw Christs day, *John* 8. 56. and did not *David* call Him Lord, when in the Spirit of Prophecy he spake of Him, *Mat.* 22. 44. and *Isaiah* saw His Glory, *John* 12. 41. And if some object, if there be so many clear Testimonies in the Old Testament of the

Doctrine

Doctrine of the Trinity, how came it to pass that now the *Jews* who have, and read the Old Testament, deny the Sacred Trinity? The Scriptures will answer you, our Saviour in the Gospel pronounces them blind, *Mat.* 15. 14. *the blind lead the blind*, and often elsewhere, and so the Apostle calls them, *Rom.* 11. 7. were they not broken off for their Unbelief, *Rom.* 11. 20. till the fulness of the Gentiles come in; and since their rejection and breaking off, the Vail is on their Eyes until this day while they read the Old Testament, 2 *Cor.* 3. 13. yet it will not follow, but that the Mystery of the Trinity was known to the Saints, and saved in the Old Testament, who believed the Covenant of Grace made with *Adam* in Paradice, *the seed of the woman should tread down the head of the Serpent*, which our blessed Saviour was to the Saints in the Old Testament, as well as to us *the Way, the Truth and the Life*, *Joh.* 14. 6. *and the same to day, yesterday, and for ever*, Heb.13.8. So that as the believing *Jews* and Church of God in the Old Testament, did believe the Doctrine of the Trinity (albeit we grant that that Mystery of the Trinity was not so clearly revealed to these Saints in the Old Testament, as it is now to us Christians under the New Testament) asserted to them in many Testimonies of Scripture; so they, reading and hearing the *Hebrew* Text, which was their Mother Language, and therein two Names of God so often joyned together *Jehovah Elohim*, the one in the Singular, the other in the Plural Number, the Holy Ghost and His Pen-men did thereby insinuate to them the Doctrine of the Sacred Trinity; and according to this, in many of the *Hebrew* Psalms, and some Spiritual Songs, there is a Doxology to *Jehovah Elohim*, closing the Psalm, to wit, these Psalms following, 76, 80, 84, 90, 92, 99, 144, 146, and 1 *Chron.* 16. 36. and *Chap.* 29. *verf.* 20. and *Psal.* 72. *verf.* 18, and 19. If then the *Jew* closed many Psalms with the Doxology to the blessed Trinity, shall not the Christian, to whom the Mystery is more clealy revealed, and in which he is baptized, and without which he cannot be saved, (for no Salvation without Christ, *Acts* 4. 12.) and he who denieth the Son hath not the Father, 1 *John* 2. 23. and as the Holy Ghost proceeds from the Father and the Son, *Joh.*15.26. so he who hath not the Spirit of the Father and Son dwelling in him is none of Christs, *Rom.* 8. 9. therefore the *Jew*, *Turk*, and *Antitrinitarian* Hereticks, who are ashamed of the Name of Christ in this Life, Christ will be ashamed of them when He comes in His Glory with His holy Angels, *Mark* 8. 38. But for us Christians, let us not be ashamed to believe and confess to our Salvation, and give Glory to Father, Son, and Holy Ghost, and with that Doxology to close the Psalm with it all our life, yea, also close our days with it on the Death-bed, following the example of that sweet Singer of *Israel*, *Psal.* 72. which he sang at the close of his days, a Prayer for his son *Solomon*, a Prayer full of comfort and faith in the Son of God, this Psalm he closes

with

with a Doxology to *Jehovah Elohim*, ver. 18. *Bleſſed be* Jehovah Elohim, *the God of* Iſrael, *and bleſſed be His glorious Name for ever and ever, and let the whole Earth be filled with His glory.* Amen, *and* Amen. So, as the *Jew* had their Doxology Glory to *Jehovah Elohim* for ever, and we have *Elohim* more clearly manifeſted, Father, Son, and Holy Ghoſt, then ſhall it not be lawful for Chriſtians to ſing Glory to Father, Son, and Holy Ghoſt for ever.

For further clearing *Jehovah Elohim*, its intimating the Doctrine of the Trinity, as I have obſerved in the *Hebrew* Text of the Old Teſtament, that theſe two Names of God when put together, eſpecially in the Prophets, are moſt ordinarily uſed (although not always) upon one of theſe two occaſions, Firſt, When the Lord is to difference and contradiſtinguiſh Himſelf from all falſe and *Pagan* gods, and then ordinarily it is rendered in the *Engliſh* Bible, *the Lord my God*, or *thy God*, or *the Lord our God*, or *your God*. Secondly, It is uſed when the Lord is giving to His Church ſome notable Promiſe of a great Deliverance, either bodily or ſpiritual in the *Meſſiah*, and ſo an evangelick Promiſe, and both theſe ways *Jehovah Elohim* intimats a Trinity, for the *Pagans* all confeſſed a Deity, but none of them Trinity in Unity. As for affixing *Jehovah Elohim* to evangelick Promiſes in the Old Teſtament, it might be the moſt proper Name to inſinuate a Trinity which was to be yet more clearly manifeſted in the Goſpel ; were it not that I intend brevity, I could inſtance both theſe, and clear them from many Scriptures in the Old Teſtament.

CHAP. X.

A Reaſon given for ſinging the Doxologie, *ſatisfactory for every Chriſtian, and that born in alſo upon the weak Chriſtian, by Sereveral Reaſons.*

I Supponed in the Preface, that the ſtrong Chriſtian and learned was ſo clear in their judgement, of ſinging the *Doxologie*, that all the former Arguments I brought, was only for ſatisfying of the weak ; and all theſe reaſons are well known to the learned ; but becauſe I know the learned does not any thing, eſpecially in the matters of God, but that for which their Conſcience is clear ; and the warrand of their Conſcience is the holy Word of God : and therefore the learned in ſinging the *Doxologie*, are perfectly aſſured that the ſame is grounded upon the infallible Word of God, or deduced from it by clear and good

good consequence, and they know that the *Doxologie* is of this nature; which reason of the strong is thus framed, whatsoever is clearly lawful from the light of Nature, and the Word of God, that to the religious Christian is lawful to do; but to sing glory to God is clear from the light of Nature, and from the holy Scriptures, therefore it is lawful for the religious Christian to do it. First, It is clear from the light of Nature, because many learned Pagans, who had no more but the light of Nature, did sing holy Hymns of praise to their gods; this is abundantly clear in Humane History, and undenyable. Secondly, The Holy Scriptures are full of it, especially the Book of the *Psalms*, commanding us to sing praises to God; now this proves infallibly the general, that it is lawful to sing glory to God: Which Conclusion being proven, I make up a second Reason, and takes the proven Conclusion for the Major; and I reason thus, It is unquestionably lawful to sing glory to God, I assume, God is Father, Son, and Holy Ghost; then it is unquestionably lawful to sing *Glory to Father, Son, and Holy Ghost*, and if any think themselves strong, and being under prejudice, are not satisfied with this reason, I would ask them if their Infant-Baptism was not an act of lawful Worship, and done in faith of the Minister that Baptized, and of their Parent that required and received that Sacrament for their use; in both which I judge the Minister consecrat and admini-

Cum tenellis Christi Agnis, & in sermone justitiæ imperitis ad ardua progredi non expediat at eruditis in Christo fortibus est abunde compertum doctrinam evangelicam de Christiani certitudine propriæ salutis a plurimis pessime abusam esse nam ut Pontificii Recedunt a veritate ex una part. ita Ecclesiæ reformatæ pars maxima, sed pessima, recedunt a veritate ex alia parte, dum nullus non impiorum crepat usque ad insaniam ipsum esse certissimum de sua salute: proinde ob hujus veritatis exactiorem investigationem & in Verbo Dei trutinatione, professores Christianismi sunt primo dividendi in verè credentes ad salutem, & in reliquos profitentes fidem ore, sed non credentes corde, quibus tamen contingit fides dogmatica, historica, vel literalis sacrarum Scripturarum in qua fide Satanas præ omnibus impiis excellit, attamen vere credentibus solis, at non omnibus certitudo salutis contingit, itaque sunt subdividendi in fortes & infirmos, infirmis in fide certitudo salutis non contingit, quia ob defectum cognitionis Scripturarum non possunt reflectere in suos actus fidei & alia fidei, τεκμηρια, quæ sunt Dei ordinaria media Christianum ad certitudinem salutis provehentia, & in particulari infirmus Christianus in cognitione puer nequit colligere suam certitudinem syllogistice, hoccine quicunque crediderit in Christum salvabitur, at ego credo in Christum, ergo ego salvabor nam infirmus in fide licet possit dicere ego credo idque vere & sincere tamen non cum ista certitu-

strat

first the Sacrament lawfully, and their Parents lawfully received them from the Laver of Regeneration, and yet I would gladly know from these that are not content with singing the Doxologie, because it is not express in Scripture, that the Christian sing *glory to Father, Son, and Holy Ghost*, why then do they not reject their Infant-baptism because it is not express in Scripture *Baptize Infants*, but well proven to be lawful by necessary consequence from Scripture, which with the universal Church we think a sufficient ground for Infant-baptism. And what is the cause that *Antipedobaptists* have fallen in that error, and separat from the true Church? Even because they were too deep in that opinion, that necessary consequence from Scripture is not sufficient warrand for an act of religious Worship, of which error ye would be aware, lest it draw you into other greater errors then you are aware of.

2. What express Scripture had *Rahab* to receive the Spies, conceal them, and send them away safely, *Joshua* 2. 9. *&c.* Heb. 11. 31. *Jam.* 2. 25. All which that she did in Faith, is proven clearly from these quoted Scriptures, then her faith was good, and acceptable to God, albeit only built on good consequences from Scripture.

3. I ask of you *John* who comes to Church, and Communicats, taking the Lords Supper, whether your worship be in faith, which I in charity suppon it is; but where

dine super quam possit fundari certitudo conclusionis, & sit cum conclusio sequatur debiliorem partem, infirmi conclusio non certo concludit ipsi certitudinem salutis, proin solus fidelis fortis in fide certitudinem salutis adipiscitur, nec hi omnes nam non pauci in fide fortes heri; hodie incidunt in flagitium scandalosum conscientiam vastantem protinus, & moraliter, & judicialiter, hesterna certitudo salutis evanescit quid quod alius non minus in fide fortis heri, incidit in deliquium solaminis hodie cum Jobo, *quod non fuit causatum peccato flagitioso; sed ob alios fines; justo, & Sancto Deo cognitos, & in Scholis Theologorum observatos: Quod ad Christianos non credentes ad salutem, est certo certius eorum nullum certitudinem salutis adipisci. Et tamen hos subdividimus in hypocritas Scripturarum sciolos, & profanos in flagitiis voluntantes, horum uterque jactat certitudinem salutis; ad diverso modo, flagitiosus dum jactat certitudinem propria salutis, novit se mentiri; at hypocritarum multi asserunt & aliqualiter gaudent in certitudine salutis, quorum error est praesumptionis; nam quod ad minorem syllogismi (*Ego credo*) sibi ipsis imponunt, nam vere opinantur se credere, licet eorum fides non sit accepta à Deo ad salutem, proinde inferunt conclusionem ego salvabor aequaliter praesumptuosam, cum assumptione, qui hypocritae in sua assumptione ego credo mentiuntur Logice, sed non Ethice.*

Christianis itaque sic divisis &

is your express warrand in your Bible, you *John*, such a man, come and worship, and take the Lords Supper as the pledge of your salvation? These words are not to be found in the whole Scripture, why then dare ye come to worship and take the holy Sacraments? I think ye will or should answer, because in the express Word of God there is a general invitation; *Come to me all ye that labour, and are heavy laden, and I will give you rest*, Mat. 11. 28. From which gracious general Invitation I suppon ye assume in sincere and good Conscience I *John* am heavy loaden, and labours to be freed of my burden by all the good means appointed by God preparatory to that holy Sacrament, which if you can truly affirm in the sight of God, then I dare assure you in the Name of Jesus that your worshipping, and communicating is in faith, albeit you have not express warrand in your Bible for you such an one by name to communicate.

4*ly*, You *John* believes to be saved, but no expresse warrand have you in your Bible, that you *John* such a one shall be saved, yet I suppon with you in charity, your Act of Faith to be allowed, and accepted of God, and to be comfortable to your Soul, for I suppone it well grounded on the Word of God, His Promise, and Command, *whosoever believes in Christ shall be saved*, John 3. 16. and *John* 6. 40. But I *John* such a one believe in Jesus Christ, therefore I *John* such a one shall be sav-

subdivisis in classes eorum pars multo minima sed tamen optima certitudinem propriæ salutis acquirit, nempe solummodo fortes & in cognitione Scripturarum, Fide & Sanctificatione, itaque ab hac certitudine removentur non solium flagitiosi & hypocritæ quin & Agni Christi teneli qua tales quin & fortes in fide aut sub deliquio gratiæ sanctificantis, aut gratiæ solaminis.

His positis inter eruditos videtur hanc questionem posse agitari num sit possibile, aut saltem probabile Christianum posse esse certum de sua salute, & eundem non esse certum de hac veritate, bonum est & expedit Christianum psallere Doxologiam Patri filio & spiritui sancto, ratio dubitationis est hæc, probavimus nullum Christianum habere certitudinem propriæ salutis nisi in cognitione religiosa scripturarum, in fide, & sanctificatione fortem: at vix est verisimile hunc fortem christianum acquisivisse certitudinem propriæ salutis, quæ veritas est difficillima acquisitu quia multum excedit lumen naturæ, & solum fundatur in lumine gratiæ, at hæc veritas Deus est licite hymno glorificandus Pater, Filius, & Spiritus Sanctus hæc propositio non solum fundatur in himine scripturarum, & gratiæ, sed etiam in lumine naturæ, ut probatum est.

Alia ratio probans certitudinem salutis esse veritatem acquisitu difficiliorem quam eam prædictam de Doxologia hæc est plurimi quibus nunquam contingit certitudo vera salutis quia impossibilis at ex eisdem non pauci qui callent sensum

eds

The Doxology Approven.   63

ed, the General Promise is express in the Word, but nor your two following Acts of Faith builded thereon, and yet you will assume they are Acts of true Faith, and for the first of the two, it's truth is best known to your selves, who are alone privy to that heart secret of yours, 1 *Cor.* Chap. 2. 11. For all within the visible Church say, I believe in Christ, according to the Apostles Creed received by the universal Church, for an Act of true Faith, and yet a great part speak not truly, This is a sad, but sure Truth, but as truely as thou believes in Christ, it is assuredly as true thou shall be saved. then if I grant that your Act whereby you believe *to be saved*, is True Faith, and rightly believed by you, albeit it is nor express in in your Bible. then why shall not this be an Act of Faith, when a Christian believes it is lawfull to sing Glory to the Father, Son, and Holy Ghost, albeit these words be not express in the Bible, altogether but deduced from the Scripture by infallible consequence, I could proceed further in this point, but because the Babes are not able to bear it, and the Learned are fully clear in this Truth, I shall not insist, and these who will not assent to the Truth, the defect is in themselves, and not in the Truth, for Children, so long as they are such, will think, speak and understand as Children, for which the strong Christian shou'd not despise the Babes, but consider they were once Babes themselves, and on the other hand, the Children

Scripturarum Literalem Historicum & dogmaticum, præcipue si in Philosophia sunt bene versati quamvis vel Hypocritæ, vel flagitiosi tamen hæc veritas, licet glorificare Deum Patrem, Filium & Spiritum Sanctum hymno facillime potest ab iis comprehendi. quia Christiani millies milleni nec ad salutem credentes in Christum nec pii, tamen has duas veritates certo credunt scilicet licet Deum hymno glorificare & hanc assumptionem, Deus est Pater Filius, & Spiritus Sanctus. & Simodo sint Philosophi nullatenus de conclusione dubitabunt, itaque possit mirum videri homines cognitionis fidei pietatis, & certitudinis propriæ salutis multum jactantes & attamen eoldem quasi sit mysterium incomprebensibile an sit licitum (vel expediens saltem) Deum Patrem. Filium. & Spiritum Sanctum hymno glorificare, dubitantes nec mirum videatur objectum fidei justificantis, & de sua salute Christiani certissimi. & hypocritæ dogmatice solum credentis, & de sua salute incerti idem esse nempe Deum Patrem. Filium, & Spiritum Sanctum; nam justificatus credit in Deum toto corde, Patrem, Filium & Spiritum Sanctum, & in Christum θεάνθρωπον sibi salvatorem, at hypocrita credit esse Deum eumque esse Patrem, Filium, & Spiritum Sanctum, & Scripturas Dei Verbum esse veras, at neutiquam credit in Deum. Patrem, Filium, & Spiritum Sanctum, & in Christum salutorem fidei justificante cor purificante, renovante, & ipsum Deo in Christo vinculo Spiritus Sancti in Æternum uniente hypocritæ fides est

L   should

should not presume, nor overwean themselves, nor judge uncharitably of the strong, but that they sing the Doxology in Faith; grounded on a strong Scriptural Consequence, as when the weak Christian *more speculativa in cerebro fluctuans at creditis ad salutem in corde radicata pieque fiducialis & practica.* takes his Sacrament, and I request the weak Christian to think soberly of himself; when *David* a Man according to Gods own heart, said in sincerity, *Psalm* 131. 2. I have quieted my self as a child that is weaned of his mother, and if ye will ask wherein he so behaved, he tells you himself he did not aspire in things too high for him. If every Christian would do so, there would be more peace in the Church.

CHAP. XI.

The Reasons why the General Assembly was not in power to lay aside the Doxology; proving their great reluctancy to their own deed, with several other circumstances alleviating the same.

IN this Chapter, we are to answer the Grand Objection, to wit, That the singing of the Doxology in the publick worship of God, was laid aside by the Generall Assembly of this Church, *Anno Dom.* 1649. To this my first answer is, that Assembly hath fourty two Sessions mentioned in the Index of the imprinted Acts thereof, but the laying aside of the Doxology is not mentioned in the Printed Acts of that Assembly, nor yet in the Index of the Imprinted Acts, therefore, seing there is no mention in the Register of the Church, to prove to Posterity, that the Doxology was laid aside, it may put some to demurr in that affair, seing there is no legal proof of it extant. 2dly. I answer, though the laying aside of the Doxology was *res gesta*, yet seing there is not a word of it in the Register of the Church, the laying of it aside, will come under the Notion of an unwritten Tradition to Posterity, 3dly. I answer, That it is to be considered whether or not the Generall Assembly was *in potestate*, and had lawfull power to lay aside the Doxology, for in their National Covenant, they grant their Religion as reformed, at the first expelling of Idolatry, and was Ratified in *Parliament*, in *Anno Dom.* 1560. And it's Confession of Faith to be Christs true and perfect Religion that they shall adhere to it all their dayes, to which they bind themselves with Solemn and fearfull Curses; but so it is, That at the said Reformation, in the Lyturgy then appointed, and Printed, at the beginning of the *Psalm Book*, *Glory to the Father, and to the Son, and to the Holy Ghost, as it was in the beginning, is now, and aye shall last*, is extant in in Prior; yea, in that *Psalm* Book of the Church of *Scotland* of the old Edition, there is great variety of the Meeter Poesies, and left any of them having their diverse Tune should want the Doxology sung at the close of it, each of these diverse Poesies have a diverse Doxology one in substance with the ordinar Doxology, but differing in some words, being framed to be sung according to the particular musical Tunes, all which Doxologies were in use in the Church of *Scotland* after the Reformation, which Book is yet extant Printed at *Aberdeen cum privilegio*, in *Anno Dom.* 1638. So that the National Covenant compared with our first Reformation engadgeth us in all *Scotland*, not to quite the Doxology, under the pain of perjury; as for that foresaid Lyturgy of *Scotland*, which was Printed, and bound in with the *Psalm* Book, it was drawn up by the General Assembly, *Anno Dom.* 1560. and 1565 and 1567.

The Fourth Answer, The General Assembly, 1639. *August* 30. Which day, that Assembly hath enacted, thus, *The General Assembly considering, that the intended Reformation being recovered, may be established; Ordains, that no Innovation, which may disturbe the peace of the Church, and make division, be suddenly proponed, or enacted but so as the motion be first communicat to the severall Synods, Presbytries, and Churches, that the matter may be approven by all at home, and Commissioners may come well prepared, unanimously to conclude with settled deliberation upon these points, in the general Assembly*: Which Act of Assembly, as it was prudently made, so accordingly practised thereafter, for in the General Assembly, *Anno Dom.* 1642. *August* 6. There are four Overtures Printed with the Acts of that Assembly to be advised by Presbyters against the next Assembly; So that this laudable Act was carefully obeyed in other things, but not so in laying aside the Doxology: For it was done abruptly, without the knowledge, or advertisement of particular Churches, Presbytries or Synods, who should have been acquainted before, and canvassed the matter, before any thing had been determined in the General Assembly anent the Doxology, and the laying of it aside, which was an innovation suddenly proponed, and instantly passed to the discomforming division of themselves from all transmarin Protestants, yea, and from the universal Church.

Fifthly, In the Solemn League and Covenant of *Scotland* and *England*, approven by the General Assembly of *Scotland*, *Anno. Dom.* 1643. *August* 17. In the said League and Covenant, with hands lifted up to the most high God, they swear sincerely, and constantly to endeavour the preservation of the Reformed Religion in the Church of *Scotland* in Worship (but then the Church of *Scotland* in their Worship did sing the Doxology,) to endeavour the Reformation of Religion in *England* and *Ireland* in Worship, &c. according to the Example of the be: Reformed Churches, but then, and to this day the best Reformed Churches did use, and still use the Doxology in the Worship of God, as is to be seen in the particular Psalm Books, in *Helvetia*, *Geneva*, *France* and *Holland*, &c. Here is the Solemn League and Covenant, are two tyes on the Covenanters in both Nations to use the Doxology.

Sixtly, The same General Assembly. *Anno Dom.* 1643. After their approbation of the League and Covenant, in their Answer to the Synod of Divines in *England* *August* 19 Writ thus, *That you may be more closely united to the best Reformed Churches in worship*, &c. But so it was, that *Scotland*, and the best Reformed Churches, did then, and to this day use the Doxology, and in another Letter of the said Assembly, to the *Parliament of England*, they writ thus, *That the Purpose, and End of the League and Covenant, is, for setling, and holding fast of unity and uniformity betwixt the Churches of this Island, and the best Reformed Churches beyond Sea*; but all these Churches beyond Seas, did then, and still does to this day sing the Doxology, then surely the Church of *Scotland*, even after their taking the League and Covenant, as it did tye them to keep the Doxology, so they sincerely purposed to keep it, and their practice was conform.

Seventhly, The General Assembly, *Anno Dom.* 1645 *Feb.* 3. *post merid.* S.ss. o By their Act, they establish the putting in execution the Directory. notwithstanding, in the close of that Act, they dissent from *England* expresly, in two particulars, anent the manner of giving the Lords Supper. As also *Sess.* 16. Of that Assembly. they freely dissent from the *Westminster Synod*, in other two particulars, as also, they provide, that this shall be no prejudice to the Order and Practice of this Church, in such particulars as are appointed by the Books of Discipline, and Acts of General Assemblies, and are not otherwise ordered and appointed in the Directory: And this Act is not only to be found Printed in the General Assembly, *Anno* 1645. But also the said Directory was Printed at *Edinburgh*, in the said Year, by Order both of Church and State, and the foresaid Act of the General Assembly of *Scotland* Printed, and prefixed to it.

Now among these particulars, in which the Church of *Scotland* preserveth her Right, and protests timously, notwithstanding the Directory, and wherein the Directory hath not appointed otherwayes, the singing of the Doxology, and the ordinar manner of Blessing the Lords People, at the close of the Publick Worship are two; for neither of which are particularly ordered in the Directory. contrarily, as for the Doxology, no mention to sing it, or not to sing it. 2dly. For the blessing of the Congregation, these are their Words, *Let the Minister dismiss the Congregation with a solemn blessing*, but no particular word of a Directory, mentioning either the blessing in the Old
Testa-

Testament, *Numb.* 6. 24, 25 Or in the New Testament, 2 *Corinth.* 13. 14. As they are both mentioned in their express words, in our *Scots* Lyturgy, at our Reformation; *pag.* 29 As also the said *Scots* Lyturgy hath the Doxology Printed in the *Psalm* Book, so that both from the National Covenant, and Solemn League and Covenant from many Acts of General Assemblies, and Letters of the said Assembly, it is without doubt and notour, that the Church of *Scotland*, when they laid aside the Doxology, were no wayes in power to do it, but on the contrare, by both Covenants, and many other previous Oaths of their own, obliged still to retain it, and not by quitting of it, so far as to have made a Schism from the Reformed Churches, with which they had Solemnly sworn to keep Union in Worship; but beside all these Tyes of their own Vowes and Promises willingly taken by themselves, which does denude them of all Liberty and Power, to lay aside the Doxology.

I bring this Reason, to wit, As the General Assembly of this Church did bind up their own hands from laying aside the Doxology, by both Covenants, and many Acts of General Assemblies beside, so there are Reasons brought from the substance of their deed to invalidat the same, as *First*, there is a Rule in the Word of God, *Whether ye eat, or ye drink, do all to the glory of God*, Then every Church Act should be done to the Glory of God, then the tenor of this Church Act must come to this, for the Glory of God, we lay aside singing Glory to God Father Son, and Holy Ghost, this is a hard saying, and like a Paradox, *For he that offereth praise, glorifieth me*, Psalm 50 13.

2dly. Consider that the Almighty can, and does make Lawes to His Creature, and His Will and infinit Goodnesse is a sufficient Reason to Him, *stat pro ratione voluntas*, but Men both in Church and State, they and their Laws both are subject to Censure, and control of the Supream Law-giver, and therefore Mens Laws ordinarly have a Rational Narrative on which they are founded, for all good Laws, are founded upon good Reasons and Reasonable Men should be led by reasonable Laws, especially when they are invalidating one former Law, or Decree, not out of use, or forgotten; but used for many Years, with approbation, yea, even to that very hour: Then this Law required a very grave and weighty Narrative, but the Act for laying aside the Doxology, had no such Rational Narrative, and in so far, it is invalidat, from having the essential of an Act, for it is like, they could not have a rational Narrative for it, therefore, it was the prudency of the General Assembly, to bury in silence both the Act, and it's Narrative; This shews their unwillingness to the thing, and therefore I hope there may the rather an Act of Oblivion, or rescissory passe upon their imprinted Act.

Thirdly, We challenge the *Romish* Church, that they lean too much to to unwritten Traditions, but I fear they may retort the Argument upon us, that some of the Reformed Church, adhere too much to unwritten Tradition, for the laying aside of the singing of the Doxology, is not in the Word of God, nor in any Act of the Church, and therefore, if there be any unwritten Tradition, owned by the Reformed Church, this must be it; For why, some people make as much dinn, and reluctance, to sing the Doxology, as some of the *Roman* Church does, for keeping of their unwritten Traditions.

4. No particular Church in this or that Kingdom hath power to change any thing in the Publick Worship of God without the consent of the Supream Civil Magistrate; stumble not at this, for it is the Doctrine of the Church of *Geneva*, (a) who also require the consent of the flock, as needful, which was granted by the General Assembly of *Scotland*, 1639. and yet in laying aside the *Doxologie* without the fore-knowledge or consent of their flocks, they went contrary to their own Act, and also contrary to the Canon of the Church of *Geneva*, for the Church of *Geneva* very orderly requires the consent of the Magistrate, and his Authority to any such innovation, but so it was that the consent of the Magistrate, so far as we can learn, was not at all required to the laying aside of the *Doxologie*, and far less was it obtained. And if that Act of the General Assembly, 1639. August 30. had been obeyed, to wit, that the laying aside of the *Doxologie* had first been debated in Synods and Presbyteries, before it had been presented to the General Assembly, 1649. (considering the many reasons which I have brought, which judicious Presbyters would have made use of) It is very probable to me that the General Assembly foresaid had retained the *Doxologie*, notwithstanding of some in *England* who desired to lay it aside, and so they had dissented in the matter of the *Doxologie* from these in *England*, as well as they dissented from them in other particulars of far less moment, notwithstanding they so much wished union.

(a) *Theses Genev. Bezæ, Anno Dom. 1586. cap. 84. Thes. 18 harum denique legum & statuendarum, & tollendarum potestas ordinaria & legitima nequit a pastoris unius arbitrio neque a solius alicujus Presbyterii judicio pendere sed accedente Christiani Magistratus consensu & authoritate cum denique & comprobante grege ista vel pom. vel aboleri debent.*

5. Having proven by many reasons the invalidity of laying aside the *Doxologie*, yet because some weak Christians have been ready to think that the General Assembly in the year, 1649 did lay aside the *Doxologie* in the Publick Worship of God, because they thought it unlawful to use it: For answer, it is a very uncharitable thought to judge of any Minister of the Gospel, and such as were members of the General Assembly, or these Divines in *England*, that they were so grossely

The Doxology Approven.

ly ignorant as to think the singing of the *Doxologie* unlawful. 2: That the General Assembly not only thought it not unlawful (for then they would have laid it aside willingly, and registrat their deed in the Books of their General Assemblies, to deterr all others from singing the *Doxologie*; but seing they left no word of it in their Register, It was because in their prudence they would not black Paper with it, far less Print it to be read by Posterity, being a deed in which they did not glory; but to the which, if I may say, they were compelled, as St. Paul speaks of himself in another case, 2 *Cor.* 12. 11. by the importunity of these in *England*, and that they might upon after considerations re-assume the *Doxologie* the more easily, that there was nothing in the Register against it.

6 That the General Assembly, *Anno Dom*. 1649. did not reject the *Doxologie*, as unlawful is thus proven; some leading Ministers who were upon the secrets of that Assembly, did thereafter without scruple sing the *Doxologie* in Family Worship, acknowledging that the Assembly did only lay it aside in Publick Worship, to please some Brethrens desire in *England*, but the laying of it aside in Families was not intended by the Synod.

7. When the Kings Majesty returned home, and Church affairs were setled, and the *Doxologie* with his Majesties express consent re-assumed, and put in practice again, then these Ministers who were present in that Assembly, 1649. and the rest of the Ministers in *Scotland*, who had all submitted for laying it aside for a time, left they should seem contentious, did more willingly re-assume it, then they laid it aside.

8 These aged Ministers who are yet alive, (for it is now 33. years past) can testifie, that that General Assembly, 1649. were far from any scruple, or thoughts of judging that the *Doxologie* was unlawful.

9. In the General Assembly, 1645. *Sess*. 15. they enact, that the Ministers bowing in the Pulpit (although a lawful custome in this Church) be hereafter laid aside, for satisfaction of the desires of the Reverend Divines of the Synod of *England*, and for uniformity with that Church so much endeared to us: that then the General Assembly declare their bowing in the Pulpit a lawful custome, then much more did they think so of the *Doxologie*, for the singing of the *Doxologie* is of much moment, it being occasioned upon a most weighty consideration, to wit the strengthning of Christians against the damnable heresie of the *Arian*, which heresie was not only damning, but also these Hereticks activity, and bloody cruelty (when they got power in their hands) did threaten the utter subversion of the true faith of the Church of Christ, therefore the universal Church spread to the ends of the earth, have ever since unanimously kept the practice of the *Doxologie*. 8. Their

8. Their laying aside of the *Doxologie* would ap
been done cordially, but because of the importunit
land, for albeit they had received the Directory, A
which time these in *England* left the *Doxologie*, w
the *Directory*; yet for all that impor unity from *Eng*
Assembly of *Scotland* did not lay aside the *Doxolt*
1649. and when it was mentioned by the Moderat
Assembly to be laid aside, Mr. *David Caldewood*,
nister of great experience, and of unquestionable it
times, spoke to the hearing of the whole Synod. *M*
that the Doxologie be not laid aside, for I hope to sing
which speech he received no satisfactory answer; a
many in that Synod by their silence did approve his f
and seasonable testimony in favours of the Doxolo,
remember that the Doxologie was laid aside by a fo
whole Synod, by calling of the Roll; only some o
gave their consent: and howsoever, the not Registr
cannot be imputed to the sloath of their Clerk; so
acquaint with these times know well that they wer
business, but fervent in spirit. But it seems strange
the General Assembly of *Scotland* in that year, 16
strong hopes of a comfortable union with *England*
gion, and upon that account to lay aside the D
them, when the General Assembly. *Anno* 1648.
at length of the perfidie of many Sectaries in *Eng a*
with *Scotland* taken the League and Covenant, and
in all its six Articles, and were hinderers of the wo
in *England*; and the General Assembly, *Anno* 1649.
now the Sectaries in *England* were the prevailing p
verted the Government, and appointed a vast toler

As for these Brethren in *England* who requeste
sembly in *Scotland* to lay aside the singing of the Do
they had taken the League and Covenant, and on t
led *Brethren*; but in that Covenant they did solemnly
Almighty God to reform Religion according to
Churches; but all the reformed Churches have still
logie, why then did not these Brethren in *England*
mark *of the truly godly*, Eccl. 9. 2. And if any woul
that they were perswaded by such strong reasons as
rate them from their Oath, in regard of singing the
swer, granting that it is possible they had such tho
"charity supposed: To which I reply, If they had
such strong reasons convincing themselves, then th
impart that new and rare light unknown to the un

more then 1300. years, they should have imparted that spiritual gift, and not hid that talent of knowledge in their Napkin, nor set their Candle under a Bushel, but on a Candlestick, to give light to all the house, not only of the reformed, but even of the universal Church.

2. It may be thought that they were obliged to clear themselves of giving offence in separating from the Reformed Churches, contrary to their Covenant, and quitting the Doxologie without so much as rendering one reason for their making a breach from the reformed Churches in their uniformity in Worship; which they did swear in their Covenant.

I am also sorry that with their quitting of the Doxologie, these in *England* did also quite both the solemn blessings in the Old and New Testament which the Reformed Church useth in the closing of the publick Worship that they would neither give God his due, nor his people; not him his solemn glory, nor them their solemn blessing, and so they have not left a blessing behind them, and it is like their way hath not been the more blessed in their deed: for as their laying aside of the Apostolick blessing, 2 Cor 13, 14. (which Text the universal Church taketh for one of the chief Texts in the Word of God for proving the great fundamental point of faith of the Sacred Trinity) So the universal Church had made use of the Doxologie these many hundred years bygone, as a strong preservative against seducing of people to errour anent the Trinity.

As for the General Assembly of *Scotland*, as they piously, and prudently, in these unsettled and reeling times, retained both the blessings of the Old and New Testament in their Publick Worship, with the rest of the reformed Churches: So it was a good presage that in the Lords good time they would re-assume and sing glory to the blessed Trinity with the rest of the reformed and universal Church, as now they do at this day, for which we give glory to the blessed Trinity.

CHAP. XII.

That invalid Scruple answered, because the Doxologie *is not to be found altogether in one place of Scripture, and the convenience of singing it proven.*

THe Apostle *Paul* as a good Pastor professeth he became *all things to all men, that by all means he might save some,* 1 Cor. 9. 22. So I am informed that some Christians weak in knowledge, because the General Assembly for a time did lay aside the Doxologie, therefore they in an ignorant mistake thought it unlawful to be sung; and they are

are promoved in that errour upon this weak reason, because the Doxologie is not express in continued Scriptures, as the Psalms of *David* are: I answer, first, If a Preacher whom they like well Preach, or Pray, or Praise God in Prose, or without a Song, although neither of these three, their Sermon, Prayer, or Praise, be express Scripture, but only according to Scripture (and I heartily wish it be alwayes so) then without all scruple they joyn in these as parts of Gods Worship, when neither that Sermon, Prayer, or Praise is the express Word of God; but if we praise God with a Tone, or Song, it must either be in the Psalms of *David*, or else it is an abomination to them: But doth not the Apostle command to praise God *in Psalms, Hymns, and spiritual Songs*, Eph. 5. 19. In which place the Learned dare not exclude any Hymn, or spiritual Song in Scripture, and we have proven already the Doxologie to be of this nature.

2. I answer, whereas they say nothing should be sung in Publick Worship but express Scripture, then let them be pleased to learn this truth, that the Psalms which they sing in Meeter or Verse, are but a Paraphrase, or short Commentary upon the Scripture for no Church nor Divine rejects the express Word of God, but for Paraphrase it is ordinary to reject one, and authorize another, as the Church finds expedient; and thus the General Assembly of *Scotland* rejected the old Paraphrase of the Psalms, as not so fit as need were in some things; and caused make a new Paraphrase in Meeter, and authorized it to be used in Churches, therefore no Paraphrase is the express and pure Word of God, so they are in a mistake singing an imperfect Commentary of mans making when they think they are singing the pure Word of God, and yet you sing it, without scruple of Conscience; then I reason that any judicious Christian understanding that all the parts of the Doxologie are either express Scripture, or so infallible Divine fundamental and saving truth, that they have been received without scruple or contradiction these 1300. years by the universal Church; so that all that time not one Christian did carp at any one word of the Doxologie; but as for the Paraphrase in Meeter upon the Psalms, as that old is rejected for its faults, so some do object and carp at some words and lines in the new Paraphrase, which ye sing without scruple; so that by consequence a learned and judicious Christian will sing the Doxologie with more clearness and contentment then some lines of the new Paraphrase; although I think that last Paraphrase any defect in it is compatible to the peaceable and moderate Christian; for this I write, not that any should reject the late Paraphrase, but that they who accept of the Paraphrase do not despise or reject the Doxologie.

3. I answer, In our Psalm Books in *Scotland*, printed shortly after the Reformation from Popery, we also printed with the Psalms some spiritual Songs and holy Hymns, with liberty to sing them in the Church;

So

The Doxology Approven.

So the Church of *Geneva*, reformed Church of *France*, and the Church of *Belgia*, have printed together with their Psalms of *David* many Scriptural Songs and holy Hymns, and have authorized them to be sung in the publick Worship of God, with the Lords Prayer. Ten Commandments, and the Apostolick Creed, all turned in Meeter, and sung in the Church; and dare any in *Britain*, who own the name of Protestant, condemn this practice of the reformed Churches beyond Seas, without the deserved reproof of Ignorance, Pride and Perversness; therefore Mr. *Baxter* in his *Method of Peace of Conscience*. pag. 411. writes thus, In my weak judgment, if Hymns and Psalms of Praise were new invented as fit for the state of the Gospel Church and Worship, to laud the Redeemer come in the Flesh, as expresly as the work of Grace is now express: As *Davids* Psalms were fitted to the former state and infancy of the Church and more obscure Revelations of the Mediator and His Grace, it would be no sinful hum ne invention, or addition, nor any more want warrand then our inventing the form and words of every Sermon we preach, or every Prayer that we make, or any Catechism, or Confession of Faith; nay it seems of so great usefulness, as is next to a necessity, and if there be any convenient parcels of the ancient Church that are fitted to this use, they should deservedly be preferred, for doubtless, if Gods usual solemn Worship on the Lords days were fitted and directed to a pleasant delightful praising way, it would do very much to frame the spirits of Christians to joyfulness, thankfulness, and delight in God, than which there is no greater care for the doubtful, pensive, and self-tormenting frame of some Christians: O try this Christians, at the request of one who is moved by God to importune you to it, *Isa*. 58. 14.

Petrus Martyr *Comment. in quintum caput Judicum* v. 1. § 4. curandum ne in templis quævis promiscue canantur sed illa tantummodo quæ divinis litteris continentur, aut quæ inde justis conclusionibus eliciuntur, & cum verbo Dei ad amussim consentiunt: nam si fenestra inventis hominum aperiatur, verendum est ne musica ecclesiastica tandem ad nugas & fabulas recidat, at approbat Hymnos Ambrosii *cani in Templis* Symbolum Athanasii & Psalmos Augustini *contra* Donatistas.

Thou shall delight thy self in the Lord, compare this with *Zeph*. 3. 17. *The Lord will rejoice over thee with joy, he will rest in his love, he will rejoyce over thee with singing*.

If it be objected that the Doxology is defective, because it expresseth not the unity of the Essence in the Godhead with the Trinity of the Persons, to wit, that we do not express glory to God Father, Son, and Holy Ghost? to which I answer, first, That it is beyond all question that these three Persons Father, Son, and Holy Ghost, are one glorious God, and so all true Christians from the rising of the Sun to its going down, do firmly believe and unanimously profess, therefore to sing it after that manner, no doubt were Orthodox; then ye will urge, why was it not so appointed at first to be sung in Churches? for answer to which question, I perceive that the *Westminster* Synod in their Directory, *Anno Dom* 1645. for Baptism, have appointed the Sacrament of Baptism to be administrate in the Name of the Father, and of the Son, and of the Holy Ghost, without adding one word more, albeit they did well know and believe that these three are one God, which no doubt they have done, following close to the example of that great cloud of Witnesses, to wit, the Universal and particularly the reformed Churches, lest otherwise they had presumed to teach our Saviour, who *is the wisdom of the Father*, to speak better and more full Divinity.

And this leads us to the chief Answer, to wit, Why the Doxology does not express the unity of the divine Essence with the Trinity of Persons, even because these ancient Doctors of the Church and Apostolick Men in their holy and due reverence given to our Saviours words, when he appointed Christian Baptism, baptizing them in the Name of the Father, and of the Son, and of the Holy Ghost; to the Doxology would neither add nor alter from that divine Pattern, and accordingly *Basil* the great writes, *Epist.* 78. We must as we have received, even so Baptize, and as we Baptize, even so Believe, and as we Believe, even so give Glory. As for the *Arian*, about the Year of Christ 350. in the Cathedral Church of *Antioch*, the *Arians* singing the Doxology, were observed to change the words appointed by our Saviour in Christian Baptism, and instead of sing-

Ecclesia antiqua fidem suam in tres personas divinas æqualis ejusdemque trinitatis Doxologiam super Christi verbis baptismi instituentis accuratius fundarunt patres concilij Constantinop. *secundi œcumen. & ab Ecclesia universali in hanc diem approbati mittunt libellum synodicum* Romam *ad* Damasum *aliosque Episcopos ibidem convocatos in quo exhibent fidei suæ de Trinitate confessionem* και ακολοθον τω βαπτισματι. *& consentaneam baptismati και διδασκεσαν ημας πιστευειν εις το ονουτα τε πατρος και τε υιε και τε πνευματ@ αγια.* Theodoret. *Hist. Eccles lib.*5. *cap.*9. *&* Nazianzen *his contemporandus oratione* 32. *Anno Dom.* 381. πιστευομεν εις πατερα και υιον και πνευμα αγιον ομοιστον τε και ομοδοξα ενοις και το βαπτισμα τηντελεκοσιν εχει, *& idem* Nazianz. *Oratione* 6. *de Spiritu Sancto* προσκυνειν πατερα και υιον και

The Doxology Approven. 75

red from Hell, yet pretending somewhat of an Angel of Light, for their heretical Spirit was seen through their Mask, in that they did not *keep fast the form of sound words*, 2 Tim. 1. 13.

ab Ecclesia Orthodoxa damnatam consule, Theodoretum *Hist. Eccl. lib. 2. cap. 24. ex* Athanasio.

Others object, To oblige Christians to sing the Doxology, is to take away their Christian liberty, who should have it still in their option to sing it or not sing it when they please? I answer, God never appointed Christian Liberty to warrand disorderly Confusion, which God disowneth; for according to this Objection, in a Church Meeting, there is one half at such a Diet that will not sing the Doxology, because of their Christian Liberty, and the other half will sing it at that same time because of Christian Liberty; and then who will deny this to be horrid and scandalous Confusion, very dishonourable to the God of all Glory, who is not the Author of Confusion, 1 *Cor.* 4. 33. and hath commanded all things to be done decently and in order; and therefore hath given power to His Church to appoint such and such things to be done decently and in order, as is clear in *Calvin*'s words.

Si Ecclesiæ incolumitati bene prospectum volumus diligenter omnino curandum est ut diligenter omnia & secundum ordinem fiant, ut cum in hominum moribus tanta insit diversitas, tanta in animis varietas, tanta in ingeniis judiciisque pugna, neque politia ulla firma est nisi certis legibus constituta, nec nisi stata quædam forma servari ritus quispiam potest, Institut. *lib. 4. cap. 10. §. 27.*

If it be objected to the Christians, to sing the Doxology so often, to wit, once at least each dyet of Publick Worship, is to make an Idol of it. I answer that defect, they who lay any weight on this Objection, it is of knowledge, to wit, That the frequent practising of any lawful Duty, in obedience to lawful Authority, is to make an Idol of it, *Deut.* 6. v. 7, 8, 9. The Lord Commands Parents to teach His Word diligently to their Children, *when thou sittest in thine house, and when thou walkest by the way, when thou lyest down, and when thou ryseth up*, &c. and inculcats, *Deut.* 11 v. 18, 19 20. Does here the Lord command to make an Idol of the Word, *Psal.* 1. 12. *Blessed is the man that meditats in the law of the Lord day and night.* is that, to make an Idol of Gods Law, 1 Thess. 5 17. *Pray without ceasing*, is to make an Idol of Prayer, then to sing the Doxology at the close of the *Psalm*, does not make an Idol of it, it being done to the Glory of God, and in obedience to lawfull Authority, and so for conscience sake. 2. Answer, It is not the frequency of the Action, that makes it Idolatrous, but trusting in the Action, although never so lawfull, and albeit, but once done; if a covetous worldling find a rich Treasure, he makes it his Idol, the first moment, so he who would give the half of his goods to the

the poor at one dell, and trust in it, as a sufficient with the Glory of Heaven, hath in so doing con Answer, A Christian may abuse any Lawful Duty and so idolize it, but it will not follow, that the is unlawfull in it self, as to give Alms to the Poo fore should not be commanded, because it may be a Trusting in any Duty is a sin of the heart, see in his neighbour, and so hath neither ability Authority. 5. Answer, Be awar that thou who Liberty, and therefore refuses to sing the Doxolo pretence of fear to Idolize it, see thou make not an stian Liberty, or of thy panick fear of Idolizing th condition, the Proverb is made true, *The fear of a* Prov. 29. v. 25. And that thou makes an Idol of th ty of Conscience, or pretended fears of the Idolizi Duty, is thus proven, that whatsoever a man prefer to God, that he Idolizeth, but the disorderly Cl maintaining of his Christian Liberty, or pretended to the Duty of his obedience to God, therefore he l stian Liberty, and pretended fear of Idolizing, for G to obey Superiour Powers in things Lawful, and cular to sing the Doxology, and all his answers is, his or fear of Idolizing forbid him to sing it, and so h obedience to God and Man, under pretence of Ido

Some say, they will not sing the Doxology, be brought it in: First Answer, This Reason is invalid the Doxology being proven, to be a good and lawfu abstain from a good Duty, because he whom you su enemy, advises you to do it: This conceit involve your own making. If your enemy, to ensnare you, will you not do it? I hope you will say you will do it then, abstain not from a good Duty in contempt of

2*dly*. Do the lawfull Duty, least your Schism, offence, I will ask you, Are you lesse oblidged to then our Saviour was oblidged to pay Tribute, b bute, least He should offend, *Matth.* 17. *verse* last.

3*dly*. The word of God commands, *if thy enem meat*, and does not the same Lord by infallible mand thee to take his meat, where he offers it, the need of it: Then let it be supposed, that provider extremity, that ye are at the point of death for hung in charity, at the Lords command offers you Meat, count him your enemy, you are bound in Conscie take his adivise, and Meat both; beware to say yo

The Doxology Approven. 77

...not help, but weaken your cause, For if you in pride
...offered, ye are your own murderer, and being a self-
...kill both your Soul, and your Body, therefore I hope hav-
...your twofold danger of Soul and Body, you will grant to
...ops Meat, for your own good, and look on him as one
...r your good in that strait, then ye will grant its lawfull
...ey the Bishops advise.
...e Bishop shall recommend it to your Paroch Pasture,
... charge of your Soul to recommend it to each Family,
...ly Worship, would you cease from the Duty, because it
...Bishop, I think you would not; and that because you had
...and then the Bishop, that made you to obey, even the
...n: Then although ye look not to the Bishops desire, to
...tology, obey the command of God, to glorifie him
...'owers of the Soul, and Members of the Body, which he
...orifie him with them; and if the Bishop exhort you to
...ay to eaven, will you refuse to do it? and I will assure
...me of Jesus Christ the great Bishop of our Souls, be-
...dgement Seat we must all appear, that notwithstanding
...ntempt of Bishops, in that day you shall see many Bishops
...n Martyrs, Confessors, burning and shinning Lights, Sons
..., and Consolation, standing in that day on the right hand
...ft, with their flocks, their Crown and joy, will you re-
...on Christs right hand, because many Bishops will be there.
...ll ye not be glad to back the Bishop in his way to glory, Ah!
...d new light will be buried in Eternal Oblivion, and the
...hts will give you an new and eternal Light, to wit, that
...ch in your Error you misjudged, as going to hell, then
...assuredly they were going to Heaven on better grounded
...u, (your scruples with which you troubled your selves,
...e in the World wherein you lived, will be all cleared, then
...oughts that you entertained of Bishops, and many other
...etter then your selves, will be blotted out of your judge-
...Eternity, and if Mr. *Calderwoods* hopes do not fail him,
...he Doxology in *Heaven*, with the Bishops: But I charge
...e not the Lambs of Christ, and truly regenerat, that ye
... to claim to this word, for it is none of yours, but the
...:ad.
...y do ye pretend your disgust of the Bishops, to be the cause
...ing to sing the Doxology, did you not refuse to sing it be-
...re Re-established, and that because the General Assembly
...whom ye obeyed, then ye refused to sing it before they
...d if they had not returned. would you have resumed it,
...vill not say it: Then if the Bishops had not returned still
...you would have refused to sing it. 6*thly.*

6tbly. I will give you better Information, ye with the rest of all this Kirk, are desired to reassume the Doxology, by Authority of the King's Majesty, for ye know it is the will of God in His Word, to invest the King with a power to restore the decayes of Religion, when they happen, and so did the good Kings of *Judah*, *Asah*, *Jehosaphat*, and *Josiah*; and accordingly our Kings Majesty, being, by the King of kings wonderfully and mercifully restored to his Crowns and Scepters, according to his duty of thankfulnesse, and Authority from the Lord given to Him, He perceiving that the Doxology was laid aside, in a time of confusion, when there was no King in *Israel*, even that part of the Kirk's publick Worship, wherein we not on'y agree with the universall, but more especially, with the Reformed Kirks; Therefore, seing all the Reformed Churches with the Universall retained the Doxology, and the General Assembly of *Scotland* laid it aside, when they were not in power to do it, therefore the Kings Majesty, by His Authority, wisely, and piously recommended the reassuming of the Doxology, therefore in refusing to sing the Doxology, ye disobey the King in that which is lawfull and right, therefore my request is to you to fear God and Honour the King, by singing the Doxology, and thereby you shall first honour God, Father, Son, and Holy Ghost, and then your King, for albeit, at the casting off the Yoke of the *Popes* usurped Power, some of the Reformed Kirks did quite the Government of the Kirk by Episcopacy, yet none of these Kirks did ever affirm, that Monarchy, or Kingly Government was unlawfull, no, nor yet Episcopacy, for albeit some of them quite Episcopal Government, because they had not Rents to sustain them, yet they granted the Government to be lawfull. I have more to writ upon this Point, but it is not for the Babes, who have need of Milk and not of strong Meat.

There remains one doubt to be answered: because the Apostle *Paul* 1 *Cor.* 6. 12. (*a*) Hath a distinction, *All things are lawfull for me, but all things are not expedient?* therefore some may say according to this distinction, albeit the singing of the Doxology be lawfull for a Christian, yet it will not follow, that it is expedient to sing it, for answer, as we have proven by many Arguments the lawfulnesse to sing it, so we shall clear the expediency which can be best cleared from the Holy Scriptures, therefore, 1 *Cor.* 10. 28. The Apostle sayes, *All things are lawfull for me, but all things edifie not.* The Greek word, which is rendered expedient, may be rendered profitable, or conducing, that is, for the Christians

(*a*) συμφερει Beza reddit conducens Pastor spiritualiter utile hoc verbum invenitur, John 16. 7. 1 *Cor.* 10. 33. 1 *Cor.* 12. 7. Heb. 12. 10. Anis. *medul. Theolog. lib.* 2. 6. 16. res media dicitur expedire cum omnibus circumstantiis consideratis ad gloriam Dei & ædificationem proximi facit.

ftians fpiritual good, and edification, but fo it is, that the finging of the Doxology to the bleſſed Trinity is moſt conducing. *Firſt,* To the glory of God, 2*dly.* To the edification of the Chriſtian, in the moſt fundamentall point of all Divinity, and this was the true cauſe, why the univerſall Church hath agreed fo unanimouſly theſe many hundred years, to retain the Doxology in the publick worſhip, and for guarding of the Lords Flock againſt *Antitrinitarian* Blaſphemous Hereticks, fo that it cannot be objected, it might be expedient then, but not now, for to the old *Arians* are now added *Socinians, Anabaptiſts,* and *Quakers,* which Errors are come to our doors. 2*dly.* If any will yet be contentious, to deny the expediency of it, we Anſwer, that the moſt competent Judge on earth to prove it's expediency, is not this, or that privat Man, nor yet this, or that privat Church but the univerſal Church, which to this day retain it, and uſe it, and therefore by their practice they declare to all particular Chriſtians, that they judge it not only lawful, but alſo expedient, which is a fatisfactory anſwer to all rational Chriſtians.

CHAP. XIII.
The many evils that flow from the refuſing to ſing the Doxology.

HAving proven the Lawfulneſſe, and Expediency of finging the Doxology, and anſwered the Doubts, and Scruples to the contrare, we ſhall haſten to a cloſe, having mentioned the evils that flow from the refuſing to ſing the Doxology, the Apoſtle *Paul,* 2 *Cor.* 1 2. 20. Mentions the evils that flowed from their divifions at the Kirk of *Corinth,* to wit, *debates, envyings, wraths, ſtriſs, back-bitings, whiſperings, ſwellings, tumults,* and all theſe are the ſad effects of their divifions, 1 *Cor.* 2. 3. That ſame Apoſtle writting to the *Galatians,* hath yet ſadder evils, *Galat.* 5. 15. *If you bit and devour one another, take heed that ye be not conſumed one of another,* which judgement I pray God in his mercy to avert from this Land, what bodily evils of Bloodſhed, Spoiling of Goods, Deſolation of Families, many Widows, and Fatherleſs Children, theſe are the ſad and ſore evils, that they are very dull and ſenſles, who takes not this to heart, but the ſpiritual evils of Sin, and Scandal is far more provoking in the eyes of the Lord, and *Firſt,* The ſin of Sedition againſt the lawfull Magiſtrat, which not only brings down the wrath of God upon a Land, but, if not repented of, ends in damnation to Soul and body, as appears, *Rom.* 13. From the beginning, another evil, the great Scandal given to the grieving of the Strong, and ſtumbling of the Weak, when they ſee the Commands of the lawfull Magiſtrat, commanding a thing ſo lawfull, as to ſing the Doxology, yet to be contemned and ſlighted, The Apoſtle

Paul, in that same place, *Rom.* 13. Says, we should obey the Magistrat, not only for fear of Gods Wrath, and the Magistrats Wrath, but also *for conscience sake*, is it not then strange Religion, when the Lord bids obey the Magistrat in all things lawfull, and that for Conscience, sake, that in the mean time, they who call themselves Christians, and conscientious will answer for Conscience sake, we will refuse to obey the Magistrat, can it here be supposed that their Conscience that will not obey, is a good Conscience, when the Conscience in the Word named, *Rom.* 13. Is certainly meaned *good conscience*, except ye will make it such Divinity as this; It is good Conscience sayes the Lord is His Word, to obey the Magistrat, in things lawful, and also according to your refusal, it is good Conscience to disobey the Magistrat therefore be pleased to consider, that there is a twofold superstition, *First* positive, which is most ordinar, to which the old *Pharisees* were much addicted; There is also a negative superstition, of which we have example, *Colos.* 2. 19 *Touch not, taste not, handle not*; there is another example of the same. *Rom.* 14 3. Where ye will find a superstitious (*eat not*) upon consideration of which two Texts, see that your refusing to sing the Doxology come not in, in that category (sing not) in which place ye may find a controversy betwixt two sorts of Christians the strong in knowledge, and the weak, the strong Christian believes that he may eat any thing, and not ask question, or scruple for Conscience sake, and him the Apostle approveth, and alloweth, for him the Apostle defends against the weak Christian, in the end of the 3. *verse God hath received him*, to wit, the strong Christian, and albeit the weak Christian, who is stiff through his ignorance to (*eat not*) yet the Apostle condemns him, because he proudly, and ignorantly thought these things unclean, whereas the Apostle sayes, they were not unclean, and therefore the strong made no scruple, but eat, and is approven of God. So in the 14. *verse* of this 14. Chapter, the weak thought that unclean, which was not unclean, and therefore refused to eat it, then apply this to your own Consciences, who sayes, (sing not) because your Conscience thinks it unlawfull to sing, when we have proven already, that it is both lawfull, and expedient; See then that ye are not as wrong with your (sing not) as these weak Christian *Romans* were with their (eat not) The strong Christian thinks it clean to sing, and dutifull, and is approven of God, ye think it unclean, and unlawfull, and are not approven of God, because ye obey not the Magistrat in that which is lawfull, and I pray you consider in the 14. *verse* of that Chapter, the Apostles vehement and emphatick expression, *I know and am perswaded by the Lord Jesus Christ, that there is nothing unclean of it self*: So I know and am perswaded with the universall Church, that the Doxology is not unclean, nor the singing of it an unclean Action, and though ye judge him that singeth, God hath saved him.

The Doxology Approven.

In these two ranks of Christians, strong in knowledge, and weak, I perceive a fault in each of them mutually toward the other, *vers.* 3. The weak judged or condemned the strong, for the Greek word κρινειν signifies both, as if they had been sinning in their eating, and as people that made no conscience of their doings: So b-ware it be not your sin proudly and ignorantly to condemn them that sings, as it were a sin. There was a sin also on the other hand in the strong that despised the weak, for their refusing to eat, because of their scrupulous and ignorant conscience; therefore it is my humble request to all that sing the Doxologie, that none of them despise or set at nought him that singeth not, upon meer ignorance, his conscience being sincere, for despising is a sin against Christian love; therefore even these who in great weakness sing not, yet bestow Christian love on them, and still the more, if ye see any sign of Christ in them, and be willing to instruct them in the spirit of meekness; for which cause I have written these lines for your information, and am to exhort you to tenderness with them in the last Chapter.

And if any object that there is some diversity and difference betwixt particular Churches which violats not Christian union, as in some Churches they kneel at the receiving of the Lords Supper, in another Church they sit, in the third they stand; I answer, albeit diverse Churches in diverse Kingdoms have divers wayes, yet no Church in one and the same Kingdom allows such a latitude as this, receive the Communion standing, or not standing as you please; but every Church have their settled way and uniformity, otherwayes it wou'd violat the Apostles rule, *let all things be done in order and decency*, 1 Cor. 14. *vers* last, and make confusion, of which God is not the Author, as it is *vers.* 33. of that same Chapter: and according (*a*) *Calvin* writes judiciously, that there cannot be order and decency unless there be one certain stated form; so that this difference in some Churches one from another, will not allow in the same Church some to sing the Doxologie, some not: For as *Calvin* did sing it to the day of his death, so neither at that time, nor never before it, was the singing of the Doxologie called in question.

(*a*) Justinianum, *lib.* 4. *cap.* 10. § 27. *Si Ecclesiæ incolumitati bene prospectum volumus diligenter omnino curandum est ut decenter omnia & secundum ordinem fiant, et cum in hominum moribus tanta in sit diversitas, tanta in animis varietas, tanta in ingeniis, judiciisque pugna neque politia ulla firma est, nisi certis legibus constituta, nec nisi stata quædam forma servari ritus quispiam potest.*

2 Answer, Albeit the universal Church hath judged some things of less moment then that the universal Church should be tyed to an uniformity in them, because Church Communion might be kept firm amongst diverse Churches, notwith-

standing that they differed in some smaller particulars; of which *Socrates* in his Church History, *lib.* 5. *cap.* 21. writes at length, which the Learned know, yet there are some things belonging to the Church of so weighty and important concernment, that the universal Church judged it no wayes expedient that particular Churches should be left to their own choise, but that the universal Church should agree upon one certain way wherein all particular Churches might keep uniformity according to the rule of Gods Word, for order, and decency, and peace; and therefore the learned know what contentions fell out in the second Century, betwixt the Church in the West, and the Churches in lesser *Asia*; for these in lesser *Asia* kept their Feast of *Easter* the same day that the *Jews* kept their Passover; but the Christians in the West kept their Feast of *Easter* upon the first Sabbath day thereafter: And albeit in this mean time the foresaid West and East Churches their judgement and practice was diverse upon that matter, yet on both sides they who were strong in knowledge still kept Church Communion one with the other, as *Socrates* proves learnedly in the foresaid Book and Chapter, so that *Polycarpus* Bishop of *Smyrna*, afterwards a glorious Martyr of Jesus Christ, albeit he did celebrat *Easter* in that same day with the *Jews* Passover, as ordinarily did all his Neighbour Bishops in lesser *Asia*, yet coming to *Rome* he Communicat with their Bishop upon their Christian Sabbath day, which differed from his day of giving the Communion at home; but because there is infirmity and weakness in many Christians, therefore after that diverse day of keeping of *Easter* raised such broils and contentions betwixt the East and West Church, that there was no visible nor feasible way for preventing a fearful rent and schism in the universal Church, until the general Council of *Nice* did appoint all to keep one day, which the universal Church hath kept ever since; therefore *Beza* in his 24. *Epist.* and 14. § thereof, distinguisheth well betwixt Ecclesiastick constitutions, some are universal, some particular, and without all controversie the singing of the Doxologie is of universal constitution; for as we have proven from antiquity of Fathers, and Councils, the singing of the Doxologie was the practice and judgement of the universal Church, therefore as the universal Church resolved to keep *Easter* upon a differing day from the *Jew*, who crucified the Lord of glory, and still blasphemes him, as *Constantine* the Great insinuats in his pious Letters after that Council of *Nice*; so that same universal Church resolved to keep the Doxologie, as a testimony against the *Arians*, and all such blasphemous *Antitrinitarian* Hereticks.

Then to apply, the singing of the Doxologie is like the keeping of *Easter* on the Christian Sabbath day, and not with the Jew on their day, to which both the Civil Magistrat by their Authority, and the Church by their Spiritual Authority did agree at the Council of *Nice*: as for that

that Text which we cited, *Rom.* 14. of Christians in two contrary opinions about meat and dayes; the Civil Magistrat nor Church had not as yet interponed their Authority, but it was still Arbitrary for the Magistrats external power, they being then all Pagans, to them both the Jewish and Christian Religion were accounted superstition about words and names, as said the Pagan Magistrat, *Acts* 25. 19. and they thought it below them to take notice of these things. as for the Church Authority, which was then Apostolick, the Learned know the reason why they did not determine these questions of meats and dayes, because there was a time allotted of *interim* betwixt the death and honourable burial of the Jews Ceremonies, which time of their honourable burial was not yet expired: and the Epistle to the *Romans* was written in this *interim*, during which time the Jewish Ceremonies of meats and dayes, &c. were *mortui* to the strong Christian Jew, and they were freed of their yoak, by taking on Chrsts easie yoak, and to the weak Christian Jew who was not clear to quite these Ceremonies as yet during this *interim* they were indifferent, and not *mortiferi*: So that place foresaid, *Rom.* 14. I fear be misapplyed by these that refuse to sing the Doxologie; for the case alters in this, the Doxologie is determined to be used both by the universal Church, and all civil Christian Powers, but these meats and dayes when St. *Paul* wrote to the *Romans*, were yet left arbitrary, therefore St. *Paul* reproved these weak Christians for their ignorance, in not eating: but how much more bitterly had he reproved and condemned them if their not eating had been a breach of the command of the Church and State, as now it is in refusing to sing the Doxologie? Yet as the singing of the Doxologie agreed upon by the universal Church differs from the keeping of *Easter* on the Christian Sabbath, and not on the Jewish Sabbath, in two particulars; 1. The universal Church did more then 200. years differ in keeping the Christian *Easter*; but all that time not one *iota* of objection or scruple against the singing of the Doxologie. 2. The Scandalizing Act of difference of keeping *Easter*, was but once in the year, but the refusing to sing the Doxologie is a scandal every weekly Sabbath.

This your refusing to sing the Doxologie, which the universal Church judgeth to be lawful and expedient, is offensive and evil both to these within, and these without the Church; for these within the Church I make this Hypothesis, that there being many thousand Protestants beyond Seas who hear that some in *Scotland* have made a separation from their Mother Church, and yet these same beyond Seas do not study the particular grounds, or pretended causes of that separation; yet these same persons being certainly informed that these of the *Scots* separation, among other differences, refuse to sing the Doxologie; which refusal of theirs is so notorious in their Publick Worship, that

It

it is like the Oyntment upon the right hand, which cannot be hid. Then what will Proteſtant Strangers over Seas conclude? Even this, that ſeing there is in *Scotland* ſome who without juſt cauſe have abandoned the Doxologie, contrary to the judgement and practice of the univerſal Church, then it is very like that their other pretences for their ſeparation are as unwarrantable; this refuſing to ſing the Doxologie is alſo an evil to theſe without the Church; which I thus illuſtrat, a *Turk*, *Jew*, or *Pagan*, being in the way of converſion to Chriſtianity; and having learned that there is one God, and three Perſons, Father, Son, and Holy Ghoſt, for in this Name he is to be baptized; and being thereafter informed that theſe ſame men who are to Baptize him refuſe to ſing *Glory to the Father, Son, and Holy Ghoſt*, in their Publick Worſhip; in what a demurr and doubtful perplexity would that *Turk* be? Or would he receive Baptiſm from theſe who were to Baptize him *in the Name of Father, Son, and Holy Ghoſt*, and yet would not themſelves ſing *Glory to Father, Son, and Holy Ghoſt*, and alſo forbid him to ſing it, would not that doubt debarr him from Chriſtian Baptiſm, and Salvation, or elſe upon better information that theſe who refuſed to ſing the Doxologie were but a han ful, who did ſeparate themſelves from the many thouſand thouſands of Chriſtians who did gladly ſing the Doxologie: Would not that *Turk* joyn himſelf gladly to that Church, whoſe Word, and Works, Sacraments of God, and his other Worſhip, was harmonious, where they did *Baptize in the Name of the Father, Son and Holy Ghoſt* did alſo in their Publick Worſhip ſing *Glory to Father, Son, and Holy Ghoſt*.

This bygone information, as I directed is only to the weak and gracious Lambs of Chriſt; yet becauſe I know there are other ſort of Chriſtians, to whom, though I owe not ſo great reſpect as to the Lambs, yet I will tender them this word, ye who refuſe to ſing the Doxologie, pretending Conſcience for your refuſing, ye are either painted Tombs, and cunning Hypocrites, or openly prophane ones who proclaim your ſin like *Sodom*. Firſt I ſpeak to the Hypocrite, thou gravely aſſevers that you dare not ſing the Doxologie, leſt you ſhould wrong or grieve your Conſcience: but how comes it to paſs that againſt thy knowledge and Conſcience thou lives in ſecret hainous ſins? wilt thou in that day when thou gives account of thy ſelf to the all-ſeeing God the ſearcher of hearts, and the eye-witneſs of thy ſecret ſins, pretend Conſcience as thy defence for thy ſchiſm now in refuſing to ſing the Doxologie, when he who is greater then thy Conſcience knows thy falſe and feigned words? Ah! thou wilt rather be ſpeechleſs then, *Mat.* 22. 12. as now thou art when thou ſhouldſt ſing the Doxologie. Therefore to prevent that diſaſter, I intreat you be not ſilent now, but ſing the Doxology, leaſt in that day, the Judge of the Quick and Dead declare, to thy confuſion, that thy refuſing to ſing the Doxology

The Doxology Approven.

was not Conscience, nor Religion, but vain Glory, Interest, Self-seeking, and Faction.

As for you who live in oppen scandalous sins, as Drunkenness Whoredome, &c. and yet dare say, we cannot sing the Doxology, because of Conscience towards God, To you, hear the Lords answer, *Psalm* 50. 16 *Unto the wicked God faith, what hast thou to do to declare my statutes? Seing thou hatest instruction, being partaker with the thief, aaulterer and slanderer*. 2dly. Doth not thy own heart smyt thee, as a mocker of God, and all Religion, when thou pretends Conscience, and when it is seared long agoe, as with a hot iron, 1 *Tim.* 4. 2. 3ly. You may indeed increase the number of your party, but you diminish their credit, then let all who pretend Conscience, depart from iniquity, and sing the Doxolowy.

When was it that the General Assembly laid aside the Doxology; even when the Army of the *English Rebells*, (who had proved false to God, in the matter of Religion, false to the King, in matter of Loyalty, false and perfidious to *Scotland*, in stead of thankfulness to them for their assistance, came in against them with the Sword, having established a vast toleration, so that, that Army was made up of the dross, and dregs, and scume of *England*, and even then, when Religion in *Scotland* and *England* was in greatest danger, then to lay aside the Doxology, was like that inference, the enemy is approaching, therefore put out your Matches, then consider the evils that immediatly, and inevitable came upon *Scotland*, after they laid aside the Doxology, what glory we lost. First, the purity of Religion, by their vast tolleration, which, with their Sectarian and Blasphemous Army, they brought Into *Scotland*; Secondly, We lost our Liberties, for no man durst wear a Sword, or Weapon for his defence, but this was a just judgement, to take a Sword from a man, when he had killed his Father.

(4) And last of all, St. *Basil* looks upon it as a fearfull prognostick, of departing from the truth, when he perceived the *Arian* not to quite the Doxology altogether, but to change it from the right words, he greatly feared a falling from the Faith to follow, so as long as ye refuse to sing the Doxology, ye continue in the begun seperation which is a fearfull evil,

(a) τίς δύναται ταῦτα ἀςενακῇ παρελθεῖν, ἢ χαρουχι πρόδηλον ἐςε και ἀντιπαιδὶ γενέθαι γνώριμον την ἀπειληθεῖσαν της πίςεως ἔκλεψοιν προοιμιαδζεθαι τα παρόντα. *Quis potest hæc absque genitu commemorare? annon ideo manifestum est, ut vel puer intelligat, hæc quæ nunc fuit esse præmia defectura fidei.*

it keeps a door open to more sin, and sorrow to follow, for by that seperation, ye keep in your heart a disgust at your Mother Church, as faulty, and assure your selves, through ye had no more Errors

rors at present, but that one, that ye refuse to sing the Doxology, yet that Error will not be alone, for Error begets in the Soul a Sinfull Inclination to more Error, as the Apostle speaks of Erronious Spirits, *they grow worse and worse* are not now too many turned Quakers, and some sweet Singers, whose beginning in Error was but small.

And to put a close to the Roll of the evils that follow the refusing to sing the Doxology. Is it not both sin and shame to offer to God a lame Sacrifice of worship, for they who refuse to sing the Doxology offer to God a lame Sacrifice of praise, and they are cursed by God, who offer to him the Sacrifice that hath blamish, when they have better and will not offer it: As for these that refuse to sing the Doxology, and think it needless, or evil, these in their heart, and by their deed condemn their Neighbour Christians, for offering to God a monstruous Sacrifice, as having a Leg more then enough, in the 2 *Chron.* 5. 13. *when was it that the glory of the Lord filled the house of the Lord, even when the singers*, verse 13. *were*, or one to make an sound to be heard in praising and thanking the Lord, but this is far from the practise of these, who will not joyn in the praises, which discord in the Lords Song, cannot be but displeasing to him: So that such practise of singing and not singing at one time, yea, worse singing and grieving at one time, for no doubt, he that sings not grieves at him that sings, and looks very like the confusion, that was after the return of the Captivity, at the laying of the foundation of the Temple of *Jerusalem*, when one part was praising and rejoycing, another part weeping and howling, and the last continued evil, Is a continued Heart-burning, and discontent in the hearts of these, who refuse to sing, and keeping a door open still for more seperation.

To close this Chapter, as Mr. *Calderwood* said, in great zeall, in that foresaid General Assembly, That he hoped to sing the Doxology in Heaven; So let no Christian think it a paradox, for the learned do know, that it may be proven by sound Divinity, for, if in Heaven, our praises to God shall be perfect (which is most surely true) then we shall praise him in all his Attributs, in all his mighty Acts, especially in his Word, and everlasting Gospel, then we shall eternally glorifie the infinitly glorious Essence, in the mysterious Trinity of the Persons; for seing in Heaven there will be neither Petition, nor Prayer, nor Preaching, which make up a great part of our worship on earth, and so all our worship in Heaven shall be praises, and that to all Eternity; and seing our knowledge of God in Heaven shall be far more perfect then it was on Earth, and then we shall see God face to face, and know him in Essence, and Persons more perfectly then we do now on Earth, and consequently, our love to Father, Son, and Holy Ghost much more perfect, so the perfection of our praises and incessantnesse, without wearing, shall answer to our greatest perfection in knowledge, and love to God, therefore it may be chriſtianly ſuppoſed that we ſhall joyn in Heaven with theſe four living Creatures, *Revel.* 4. 8. who reſt not day nor night ſinging, *Holy, Holy, Holy Lord God Almighty, who was, and is, and is to come*; where was this *triſagium* uttered, The firſt two Verſes of this Chapter affirm, that it was in Heaven, who were the living Creatures that kept this *Chore* of *laus perennis*, the Aſſembly Notes upon it, ſayes, it was the Miniſters of the New Teſtament. 3dly. What was the ſubject of their praiſes, the Aſſembly Notes ſay, they continually praiſe God, and ſet out the Trinity of the perſons in the God-head.

If any pleaſe to object, the Church appointed the Doxology to be ſung, to guard the Flocks of Chriſt againſt *Antitrinitarian Hereticks*, but in Heaven there is no danger, for no Devil, nor *Antitrinitarian* will be there to tempt, and the glorified Saints will be made perfect in Holineſſe, I anſwer, when *Iſaiah* 6. 2, 3. The *Seraphims* cryed one to another, by way of Anthem, *Holy, Holy, Holy is the Lord of hoſts, the whole earth is full of his glory*, Here I hope was neither *Arian* nor *Antitrinitarian*, yea, I affirm, according to the *Seraphims* ſinging a Doxology to the Trinity, that although there had never been *Antitrinitarian Heretick*, nor danger of Devils to tempt them to that hereſie, ſeing the Angels in Heaven did ſing a Doxology to the bleſſed Trinity, which is granted by the univerſal Church, then ſhall it not be lawfull, expedient, and comely for Chriſtians to ſing Glory to Father, Son, and Holy Ghoſt, whoſe motto in Baptiſm, is to be Baptized in Name of Father, Son, and Holy Ghoſt.

Therefore, to conclude this Chapter, theſe who have Scruple, or Doubts to ſing the Doxology for want of knowledge, my prayer is to God, Father, Son, and Holy Ghoſt, who is the Father of Ligh's, to reveal even this unto them, that we may with one Mind, and with one Mouth glorifie God, even the Father of our Lord Jeſus Chriſt, *Rom.* 15. 6. Now to God, Father, Son, and Holy Ghoſt be glory in the Church, by Chriſt Jeſus throughout all Ages, world without end *Amen. Epheſ* 3. *Chap.* at the laſt *verſe.*

CHAP. XIV.

An exhortatory Conclusion to the strong and orderly Christian, to receive and imbrace with all Christian love and tenderness every weak Christian, who shall return from their wandring in Error, to live in Order and unity in the Bosom of their Mother Church.

BEing now to conclude this little Treatise, As its scope and aim is for healing and helping home of the wandring Sheep, so my work in this Chapter is to remove all Stones and Stumbling-blocks out of the way of the weak Lambs returning to their Folds again; and I beseech you, put not the blame so much upon these Lambs, as upon these Men who drew them away and misled them; and let all good Christians rejoyce in their return, and welcome them home, and that because of the manifold Evils that this Kingdom was groaning under, which now God in His Mercy hath almost removed: Was not in many Families the Father against the Son? and a Man's Enemies these of his own Houshold? did not many Flocks forsake their Fold and resting Place, and strayed in the gloomy and dark Day? was not the empty Walls of many empty Paroch-Churches mourning? and the Stones of emptiness crying out? and Pastors lamenting that their Flocks were departed? and a few left? yea, sometimes the Pastor so evil intreated, by his Flock turning Wolves, that he must needs convey himself away out of that place, some being spoiled, some wounded, some killed, some like desolate Widows mourning in secret in a desolate Retirement, like *Jeremiah* in his wished Cottage in the Wilderness, *Jer.* 9. 2. and for a long time the Magistrate loath to use rigour, which made them the more inexcusable, and at last they display an open Banner of Rebellion, whereby they wilfully run themselves into a Labyrinth of Miseries, to be killed and spoiled, and many impoverished, and not a few suffered death by the hand of Justice, whose infatuate Souls (with that sour leaven of their dangerous Doctrines) was at their death a far more sad spectacle to the Godly then their bodily death, which remembers me of *David*'s bitter mourning for his traiterous son *Absalom*'s death; and this Malady and sore Disease came to so great a height, that it threatned death, which was more then once prevented by opening of a Vein, and many thought our Disease incurable, and that it would turn at last to be a rooted Hectick to the consuming of the Marrow; but blessed be our kind *Samaritan*, who beyond the expectation of many, and much more beyond our deservings, hath pitied us, for it was a time of love, and when we were lying in our Blood, he said Live, again he said Live, *Ezek.* 16. 6. even when the Enemy was saying there is no help for him in God, yet he hath poured in Wine and Oyl in our Wounds, and letten us (by sweet experience) know that there is both a Physician, and Balm in Gilead; and the God of our Health hath rebuked that Feaver, and hath commanded and created deliverance: Then let every one of us rejoyce in God, and count it our glory to be workers together with God: Is this a time of healing? let us concur and contribute our help; Is the Lord's Flock returning? then cast up, cast up, gather out the Stones; Hath the Lord Jesus awakened out of sleep, and rebuked the Winds and Seas, so that now there is a great Calm, then let us all help to row to bring the Vessel to a safe Harbour; when the Lord is bringing back the captivity of His People, let our Mouthes be filled with laughter and our Tongue with singing; behold and see, not one Dove alone returning to the Ark of their Mother Church with an Olive branch, *Gen.* 8. 11. but a whole cloud of these Doves are flying to their Windows, *Isa.* 60. 8. Are not the Pastors returned to their Flocks with joy who went away weeping, returning with the full blessing of the Gospel of Christ, now to bring forth the peaceable fruits of Righteousness of their sad and desolate retirement and widow-head, *Lam.* 3. 27, 28, 29. like St. *Basil* returning from the Desart, and St. *Athanasius* from his Exile; and now that promised Blessing shall be given them, *Isa.* 30. *v.* 29. *your eye shall see your Teachers.* And now my Brethren, who had precious retirement to read, meditate and pray, and a sad cross to put you to it, then with *Timothy*, 1 *Tim.* 4. 15. *let your profiting appear to all.* Ye know what *Luther* writes, Prayers, Meditation and Temptation made good Theologues, and the Flocks that have been misspending their time, had the more need to redeem the time.

Now I turn my speech unto you in this Church who are strong, and have overcome that evil one, and have obtained Grace to live orderly before God and His Church during the time of these Confusions; as your compassionate Souls did grieve for Sin, weep in secret before the Lord to enlighten, inform and reform them, to reclaim and reduce them, therefore hath the Lord given you a gracious return of your Prayers, in returning them; then open your loving Hearts, and embrace them, and these hands that were with outstreached arm lifted up to God for them, let your arms embrace them, and by word and deed, and contenuance, express the sincerity of your love to them, and as the Lord hath given you more knowledge then to them, let it be your generosity not to insult over them, or despise them, but with all tenderness not to look down, but to stoop down to their Weakness, and let the strong elder Brother stoop down with his Hand, to hold by the hand or arm, a younger Brother learning to Walk, and count it his Glory to speak with him in his own childish Dialect, and take little steps with them; then I beseech you in the bowels of Jesus, reproach them not for bygones, but pass an act of Oblivion, and in time coming, use all gentleness and forbearance, and so gain them to love you; and in all things indifferent and undetermined if he be not clear for the one way, condescend to him and follow his way; bear with his infirmities, rashness, incivilities and ignorances, and others overweaning themselves as if they were strong in Knowledge; this is an infirmity of many weak, and yet for Peace sake, the strong ought to bear with it: Now this Duty of the Strong in bearing with the Weak, the Lord presseth much in His Word, *Rom.* 15. *v.* 1, 2. Why hath the Lord given thee more Knowledge, Mortification, Patience, *&c.* then to the Weak, but for this end, to bear with their Infirmities? for their Spiritual good, for which St. *Paul* gives you his holy example, 1 *Cor.* 9. 22. *For the weak became I as weak, that I might gain the weak; I am made all things to all men, that I might, by all means save some*: and *Chap.* 10. *v.* 33. *I please all men in all things, not seeking my own profite, but the profite of many, that they may be saved*: Here is a great *placebo*, and yet no Flatterer, but in his converse acceptable both to God and Man. The Spirit of Christ is not a sowre, censorious, sullen and carping Spirit, but meek, gentle and easie to be intreated. When the Child as yet but an Intrant in the World, and learning to speak, will ask the Parents some childish question, will the Parents be incensed to inflict Chastisement, or rather will they not pass it with this Meditation, *when I was a child, I thought as a child, I understood and spake as a child,* 1 Cor. 13. 11. So, if any weak Babe in Christ propone or start any question in Religion (to which many Babes are too ready,) do not think that ye are always bound in Conscience to answer them, for many times our Saviour did it not, *Act.* 1. 6. *Jo.* 21. 20. And the Apostle to *Timothy* speaks of foolish and unlearned questions, which produce strife and no edification, 1 *Tim.* 6. 4. then let the strong wave the question with a general answer, *Jo.* 16. 19. or instead of speculation leading to practice and holy life; *Luk.* 13. 23. Yea thirdly, It may be waved if it be beyond the sphere of the Larger Catechism, for Questionators that furnishes their common Discourse with Questions are unsavoury company to the Godly, and the weak Christian should not be entertained by the strong Christian with Questions; it is expressly against the Apostles rule, *Him that is weak in the faith receive ye, but not unto doubtful disputations,* Rom. 14. *ver.* 1. then let neither strong nor weak Christian (especially in Company) move any question of Religion, especially these that belong to the present Differences, least the Strong touch the Weak on the old Sore, and so but grieve and irritate, which no doubt grieves the Spirit of God, and is not the healing way: As for the Weak, I intreat them who have been wandring in Mistakes, to resolve in the strength of Christ, in all time hereafter, to live orderly as to the Church, and

loyally

loyally as to the King and Rulers under him, and then he is a cursed Man that will not be loving and kind to thee.

Then let the strong imitat their Father in Heaven, who when his pro.ligal Son returns, no word of his sin (with which the elder Brother did upbraid him) but ran, and met, and kissed him, gave him new cloaths, and shoes, adorned him with a Ring, feasted him and made merry, *Luk.* 15. 20. *He ran and met him, and fell on his neck and kissed him,* and imitate the Son of God, the great and good Shepherd, who brings home on his shoulder rejoycing one wandering sheep, does he not rejoyce much more now then in reduceing so great a flock?

And the Fathers kindness to his returning Prodigal, is so sweet a subject, that I delight to mark in it further, that when the elder Brother uncharitably endeavoured to exasperat his Father against his younger Brother, calling up his old sins, the Father rejects the elder Brothers bitter Libel: See both the last and 24. verses, his *Brother was dead; and is now alive, he was lost, and now is found*; Its gemination shews Emphasis, he was lost when dead in sin, but now alive to God to righteousness; he was the lost and wandering Sheep, he is come home a penitent sinner: And compare the 24. verse with the last yet more, my Son thy Brother he is sibb to thee, but sibber to me, which the words imply; therefore though ye would let him go as he came, yet will not I, O dear younger Brother be not afraid to return, nor scarr to come home, but first see that thou make thy peace with thy Father, *verse* 21. And although some churlish elder Brother (like *Eliab* to young *David*) would unchristianly chide thee, take courage, it is not that bitter Brothers house thou art coming home to, but thy Fathers; meditate and think on these things, for to be a ready antidote against the bitter Pills of some; and albeit some of the stronger Brethren be not so kindly, comfort thy self, here is thy Father pleading for thee, and so is thy elder Brother in this same *Chap. Luke* 15.6. who when he hath brought home his wandering sheep, rejoycing calls together his friends and neighbours, and sayes, rejoyce with me: then assure thy soul that Christs real friends will rejoyce at thy return, welcome thee, imbrace and love thee as their own bowels.

Then let us in this great act of charity, and tender love to the weak returning Lambs, imitat our blessed Redeemer, and elder Brother, who came from Heaven to Earth to seek and save the lost sheep, *Luk.*19. 20. who *bears the Lambs in his bosome, and leads them gently that are with young,* Isai. 4. 12. and will be more loath to over-drive them then *Jacob* his young Children and Flocks, *Gen.* 33. 14. Then be thou compassionat towards them: Is the Saviour bearing them in his bosome? then grieve them not, for he cannot but see it, and be grieved. Is he leading them gently, then dare thou beat them back with word or reproach, like the piercings of a sword?

The

The Lord leads the lame and the blind in the way they do not know to Zion weeping, the woman with child, and she that travelled with child, *Jer.* 31. 8. Mark the four sorts in the world, the fittest objects of mans compassion, and help lame and blind, the woman with child, and travelling with child; and the first two most despicable, yet the Lord despises none of them; but seeing they are weeping and coming to Zion, he is eyes to the blind, and legs to the lame; therefore strive thou so to do with holy *Job,* 29. 15. And beware on the other hand to deserve the curse for laying a stumbling block before the blind, or make them wander out of the way, *Deut.* 27. 18.

Is our blessed Saviour binding up that which was broken, strengthning that which was sick? *Ezek.* 34. 16. *For he will not break the bruised reed, nor quench the smoaking flax,* Mat. 12. 21. Then thou strong Christian follow that same trade, strengthen the weak hands, and confirm the feeble knees of these Lambs.

Did the Son of God assume soul and body, flesh and blood, that he might give his flesh to feed his Lambs? and charges *Peter* as he loved him, *feed his Lambs,* Joh. 21. 19. And what kindness thou shews to his Lambs, in the day of thy accounts he will count it up to thee as done to himself, *Mat.* 25. 45. Lay hold of this opportunity as a good Mercat to imploy to the uttermost all thy talents of gifts and graces, lay them out in helping to bring home the Lambs of Christ, and in learning to bear with the infirmities of the weak Lambs: Look to thy perfect copy that hath no blot in it, *Joh.* 3. *vers.* 1. and downward, what pains our Lord takes on *Nicodemus,* bearing with his rudeness and weakness in knowledge, though some of his Questions were most childish; but our Saviour will not put out the spunk of his smoaking flax, which kept kindling from that time forth, for he pleads Christs cause behind his back, *Joh.* 7. 5. And as a true believer his faith kythed when the Apostles were weaker in faith, durst not be seen, nor kyth; and with *Joseph* of *Arimathea* waited on Christ at a dead lift, and with living faith helped to enbalm and bury his Saviours body: What knows thou but some of these weak Lambs whom now thou helps to come home, but hereafter when they grow stronger they may help thee at a dead lift: Our Saviour did decree it, and foresee it in *Nicodemus,* no doubt, but thou can do neither.

The woman of *Samaria, Joh.* 4. 7. when our Saviour is hungry, thirsty, and weary, about mid-day, after his journey, she not only refuses him a poor drink of water, but checks him for requiring it; notwithstanding he did not only bear with her uncivility, but also he offers her better water; which she not only refuses, but gives him two checks in stead of thanks for his offer: but he who did bear our sicknesses, did bear with her infirmities, although he said, *How long shall I be with you? how long shall I suffer you;* and this was a part of his

pennance

ennance for thy fins: then thou proud worm, shall thou storm or murmer at thy Lords command and example, to bear with the infirmities of the weak.

It is probable thou will propound this doubt, shall I show all that kindness to these of which I may have probable grounded doubts that they are not gracious? For answer to thee, thou art not a fit Judge of hearts; if their Lord and thine hath bestowed on them the priviledges of the visible Church, and they profess faith in that same Saviour with thee, then he allows thee to judge charitably of them, and converse with them in Christian fellowship, and love; yea, doth not our Lord, *Mat.* 9. 10. who hates all workers of iniquity, *Psal:* 5. 5. as such, yet he did converse with them, he condescends to eat with Publicans and sinners, as their spiritual Physician, who loved mercy better then sacrifice; for the prudent Physician will bear with many morosities in speech and behaviour from his Patient, and all for their good, intending their health: And if some would object, granting it to be a point much belonging to the Physicians Calling and Trade, yet they doubt if ordinary Christians be so tyed. I answer, Thou art as strongly bound as he by thy Christian Calling, *bear ye one anothers burden, and so fulfil the Law of Christ,* Gal. 6. 7. Rom. 15. 1. The great Physician will examine thee upon this his Law, as well as the Physician upon his Cures: for thou wilt find in the day of thy accounts, thou will be as well examined how thou imployed thy Talents of knowledge, mortification, patience, and charity, in winning and strengthning thy weak brother, as well as the Physician how he imployed his skill for healing of his sick Patients: See how the Creator of Angels condescends to converse, eat and drink with Publicans and sinners, to the admiration and ignorant sinful stumbling of the proud Pharisees, these whited Tombs: See and admire how that Lamb of God admits that woman, a great sinner, known for such in all the Town she lived in, *Luk.* 7. 39. to kiss his feet without ceasing, when *Simon* the Pharisee in the mean time, who had invited Christ to dinner, wondered that such a holy Person suffered such a vile sinner to touch him, but the Pharisees were utterly ignorant of this Doctrine, the strong to stoop and support the weak, and their Satanical pride made them uncapable of it, for our Saviour who knew what was in man, describes them, *Luk.* 18. 11. They trusted in themselves that they were righteous, and despised others, which two sins are inconsistant with true Grace: then let the strong Christian beware of these two sins: and thus hitherto we have set before the eyes of your Soul the blessed example of our blessed Redeemer, then I beseech you, who are strong in Christ, by the meekness and gentleness of Christ, that ye bear with the infirmities of the weak Lambs, and count it your glory.

But it is probable, that some unwilling to this Duty, will strive to
thus

shune the yoak, as being absurd, and so no binding Duty, why, say they, to bide the strong counterfite, and dissemble, and fain themselves to be weak, when he is strong; I answer, their is a great difference betwixt simulation and dissimulation, for the first is lawful, and our Saviour practized it, *Luk.* 24. 28. *Christ made as though he would have gone further*, *Beza* renders it (*fingebat*) which I like not so well, the Syriack Interpreter (*faciebat eos putare*) But *Aretius simulabat*: For clearing up of this Christian policy of simulation, for the good of the weak Christian, *First*, Al the time our Saviour was upon the stage of this World, did he not hide the glory of his divine Nature, under the Rags of the mortality infirmities, and misery of His humane nature, *Isaiah* 53. 2, 3. *He hath no form nor comliness, there is no beauty, that we should desire him*, verse 4. *we did esteem him stricken, smitten of God and afflicted*, for he did not manifest His Glory, but only to his own, and that only in some degrees, as, and when it pleased himself, *John* 1. 14. And when the two Disciples were going to *Emmaus*, *Luke* 24. 16. their eyes were held that they did not know our Saviour, who dare challenge any fault here? And when a Christian in his lawfull actions propones moe ends then one, which is lawfull for him, it is lawfull for him to conceall some of these ends, that the King of kings condescends to mans weak capacity, as if he had eyes, ears, hands, feet, and passions, when all these are infinitly below his purity, and perfection, so the Parents and Nurse speaks such broken language to the Babe, as it best understands, and the end makes it lawfull, the childs edification, and this same makes the condescending of the strong to the weak lawfull and acceptable, *Rom.* 15. 2; *Let every one of us please his neighbour for his good to edification*; yea, St. *Paul* caught the *Corinthians* with guile, 2 *Cor.* 12. 16. All Trades have their secrets, so practical Divinity, and many cases of Conscience: therefore *Augustines* answer upon this question, in his 19. *Epist.* that these simulatious, and stoopings of the strong to the weak, is not *mentientis, astu, sed compatientis affectu*, but that same Apostle 2 *Cor.* 11. 29. seems to aggravate this doubt, *who is weak, and I am not weak*, then St *Paul* is really weak with the weak, which seems *repugnantia in adjecto*, when he was really strong, both in Knowledge, Faith, and Holiness, how then was he weak? I answer, through compassion, and the more strong in Sanctification, the more sympathizing, and compassionat, his Soul the more wounded with sorrow, and so the weaker through compassion, and that in two conditions, First, to apply to the strong Christian, are some returning cordially to live in peace, and order, and thou seeing them weak, be weak with them, stooping to them, taking half steps with the weak Lambs, and not thy own strong long steps, are they now shortly recovered out of a dangerous sickness, be very anxious that you occasion not them to relapse, was their foot disjoynted, is it now set right?

right? then help them to take easie and even steps; there is another sort not yet come to land, but on a Ship broken plank wearing to shoar, let thy Soul be weak for them, fearing and dreading their sinking, and be using all good means to bring them safe to land, the Mother though in good health, if she see her Child weak, and in danger of death, in her compassion will she not turn really weak, and be at the sowning for fear and grief.

As we have set before you the example of God, and Jesus Christ our Peace-maker, so we shall presse the Duty, being so acceptable to God and good men, with moe persuasives, and first, seing there is no gaining of our neighbours spiritual good so readily, as by gaining their love first, for then, and not till then will they take advise, or information, willingly, and therefore, the most effectuall way to gain them from their Error, is, to perswade them of our love to them, which is only best accomplished by loving kindness, and carriage towards them, for no man will take advise, information, or counsell from him whom he suspects, or thinks to be, his enemy.

2dly. Thou art obliged in Conscience, in thy judgement of charity to look on him as an Elect, it may be as reall as thy self, then if thou have that charitable judgement, to think thy self Elect also; I. in the name of him who hath elected you both, charge you to be kind to him, especially, if you were in Christ before him; see what kindnesse *Judah* an strong elder brother, many wayes bestowed on his younger and weak brother *Benjamin* Gen. 44. 33. *I will be a bond man to my lord, and let my younger brother Benjamin go home to his father.* what knows thou, but thy weak brother may be the beloved *Benjamin*? therefore use, and improve all thy gifts, and graces to bring home that darling *Benjamin* to his Father and thine.

3dly. Look upon thy weak Brother as dear to Christ as thy self, even the price of his Blood and Death, consider, *Rom.* 14. 15. and 1 *Cor.* 8. 11. And therefore beware of that fearfull sin of destroying thy weak brother for whom Christ dyed, by thy stubbornesse, and unkindnesse to him, be aware to give him a sower look, or down look, thou little knows, how little a stone will cause his weak foot to stumble.

4ly. Look upon thy weak Brother as a Member of that same Mystical Body of Christ with thy self, 1 *Cor.* 22. 17. Where the eye cannot say to the least Member, the finger, or toe, I have not need of thee, *verse* 20. But on the other part, when the weakest, or smallest toe of thy foot is hurt, will not the Mouth cry, I am hurt, and suffer with it, and seek Cure, *verse* 16. The hand will apply the salve, and the eye see that it be well and right done, then if thou be a well seing eye, and have but a little sore toe, yet he is a Member of that same Mysticall Body of Jesus, who will feel his sore, and cure it.

P

5dly.

5thly. Christ Jesus is head of all that Mystical Body, whereof both that weak Lamb and thou art Members, and he is a feeling and compassionate head, *Ephes.* 4. 15. And thy kindness to the weakest of his Members, he will take it and repay it as done to himself, If thou edify in love the least Member of his Mystical Body, *Ephes.* 4. 12. Or if thou despise, and hurt the weakest of these his Members, will not that Glorious Head, whose eyes are as a flame of fire, *Revel.* 1. *verst.* say, *I have seen, I have seen.* Exod. 3. 7.

6thly. Look upon thy weak Brother, as a living stone in that holy and spiritual Temple, whereof Christ is the foundation, and chief corner stone and Christ also the Master-builder, commands thee who are strong to polish thy weak Brother, and build him up in the Faith, 1 *Pet.* 2. 5.

7thly. Consider him as a little Temple to God, 1 *Cor.* 6 19. Then for thy Lords sake, who dwells in it, help to polish and adorn it untill the Cape-stone be put on, this do at his command, who might have left thee in thy natural condition, a leprous stone, and cast thee into that unclean place without the City *Levit.* 14. 40.

8thly. As the whole body of Believers are Christ's Bryde, and Spouse, his Sister, his Dove, his Undefiled, then this same Relation hath every particular Believer to Christ; Therefore help to deck and adorn his Spouse (the weaker the more tenderly) as a Bride prepared for her Husband, let her not have cause to complain to her Husband, that instead of adorning thou did rather rob and pull off.

9thly. Beware to disdain that younger Brother, for his weakness, and infirmity, and ignorance at present, what knows thou, but for all that he may redeem the time, and overtake thy self, and run by thee and prove a stronger Christian, and greater Saint, first on Earth, and then in Heaven nor thy self.

10ly. As truly as in nature thou was a Babe, before thou was a Man in strength and stature, so in Grace and Knowledge thou was once a Babe, and it may be profane also, which motive St. *Paul* presseth, *Tit.* 3. 2, 3. *Be gentle, shewing all meekness to all men, for we our selves were sometimes foolish, disobedient, deceived, serving diverse lusts and pleasures,* but it may be thou will say, but I was never disloyal to my King, I answer, thank God for his good providence in thy good education, in regard of Loyalty, but has thou not been disloyal to the King of kings, by many wicked lusts?

11thly. What knows thou, but ere thou die, thy Soul's condition may be as pitifull and low, as the weakest Lamb, that now thou seest returning to the Fold, what knows thou, but thou mayst fall in scandalous and grievous sin, and thereby be brought to the very brink of disspair, or with *Job,* in a desertion crying, *pity me pity me, O my friends for the hand of God hath touched me, Job* 19. *Chap.* 21. This motive is pressed by St. *Paul Galat.* 6. 1. *Brethren, if any man be overtaken in a fault, ye that are spirituall restore such an one in the spirit of meekness, considering thy self, least thou also be tempted.*

12*thly* If thou be obliged in Conscience to lay down thy life, for thy Brother, 1 *John* 3. *verse* 6. then certainly it is chiefly for the good of his Soul, even as Christ laid down his life for him, then thou art strongly obliged to do the lesser Dutie for thy weak brothers spiritual good, even to be kind and compassionat toward him.

Hath not the Lord put it in the heart of the most cruel Tyger, and devouring Lyon to be kind, and loving to their young ones, and the Reason is the same. In the general, the Parents are strong, and their young Ones weak, and has need of their help, and that Law of God in nature is obeyed, the Lyoness gives suck to her young weak Ones, and the Sea-monster draws out the breast, and gives suck to their young Ones, *Lament* 4. 3. So thy Lord commands thee who art strong to help thy weak Christian Brother.

¶ Yea, does not the whole building of Heaven and Earth keep inviolable, by these Laws which their, and our Creator gave them, for their own particular, and mutual preservation, First, the Earth furnisheth Fewel to feed the fire, and entertains it in its bowells, as appears in many Countries. 2*dly*. The Earth keeps also in its bowells the treasures of wind, which by their blowing, help to keep both Air and Water from corrupting. 3*dly*. The Sea furnisheth the Earth with Water, sending it up to the Clouds, and they down to the Earth, and by conveying Water through the bowells of the Earth to furnish continuall springs on the tops of the highest mountains. 4*ly*. Does not the stars send down their influences many hundred thousand myles from Heaven to Earth, and rules the four Seasons of the Year, *Job* 38. *verse* 31. 33. Yea, the Sun and Moon send down their influences, not only much conducing to the welbeing of Man and Beast, but also to the vegetables, *Deut.* 33. 14. Precious Fruits brought forth by the Sun and Moon, yea, their influences pierces to the bottom of the Seas, and bottom of the Mountains; So in this lower World, the King of Saints hath a City His Temple, His House, and every Believer is a stone thereof, to which City this King of Saints hath given Laws, even that the strong and able Citizen, shall help to build the weak, that they may be still the more firmly united to Christ the Foundation by stronger Knowledge, and Faith, and better polished by more holy Life.

As this Duty is great and good, so many Graces are required in the Soul of the strong, for performing this Duty to the weak, and first, Christian love, for knowledge puffeth up, but thy charity will edify thy weak Brother, 1 *Cor.* 8. 1. *It suffereth long, is kind envyeth not, vaunteth not it self, is not puffed up, doth not behave it self unseemly, is not easily provoked, thinketh no evil, hopeth all things, endureth all things,*

1 Cor. 13. 4. If thou then have this Charity to thy Brother, how sweet a converse will it procure betwixt thee and thy weak Brother. The second Grace Humility, *1 Pet.* 5. 5. Cloathed with Humility, in lowliness of Mind, each esteeming other better then himself, *Phil.* 2. *v.* 3. Thirdly, Meekness, *Phil.* 4. 5. Gentle shewing all Meekness to all Men, slow to Anger, if thou be of great understanding, *Prov.* 14. 29. a greater Vassalage to thee then if thou hast taken in a City, *Prov.* 16. 32. which three Graces are joyned together, *Ephes.* 4. 2. and *Coloss.* 3. 12. as beseeming Graces to the Elect, and especially to Church-men, who should be of the strong Christians that we are speaking of, whose office is to please the Flock for good to their edification, 2 *Cor.* 13. 10. and should do all things for their edifying, 2 *Cor.* 12. 19. gentle to all, in Meekness instructing these that oppose, 1 *Tim.* 3. 6. And here I will speak a little to my reverend Brethren of the Ministry, especially to these who have had the most grieved hearts for the wandring of their Flocks, and now finds their comfortable return, I hope I need not press you to loving kindness toward them, for I think every good Minister of Jesus Christ in this *juncto*, will be so overjoyed, that he will rather incline to the other extremity of indulgence to them who return, and will be far from all tartness and sourness towards these returning Lambs of his; and albeit hitherto they have possibly miscarried to thee, by word or deed, yet seing their Father & thine hath forgiven them the ten thousand Talents and thee also, then likewise must thou Christianly forgive the small Mites of Offence which any of the Flock have committed against thee, remembring these words of great St. *Basil*, who endured the heat of the day, in the time of the *Arian* Persecution and says, that Church-men of all other would be most abominable, if they did not love the reuniting of the Members of Christ's Mystical Body before all Earthly things, yea, and himself wisheth the reunion of the Church more than his own life.

Καὶ γὰρ ἂν εἴημεν πάντων ἀνθρώπων ἀπαολοι ὀχισμασι καὶ καλαιομαις εκκλησιων σφοδομενοι καὶ μὴ τὴν συνάφειαν των μελων τε σωματος τε χριστε το μεγιστον αγαθων τιθεμενοι.

Sane quidem essemus omninum mortalium absurdissimi si schismate & distractione Ecclesiarum oblectaremur nec membrorum Christi corporis coalitionem ante omnia alia bona reputaremus Tom. 2. epist. 342. *Idem* epist. 265. *initio* ἂν δὲ τῆ καρδία μὲ τοσαύτην ἔχειν επιθυμιαν φημι ειρηνευθαι τὰς εκκλησίας ὥσε ἡδέως ἂν καὶ τὴν ζωὴν τὴν εμαυτὲ πρέσθαι ὑπὲρ τὲ τὴν ὑπὸ πονηρε ἐξωσθεῖσαν φλόγα τὲ μίσες κατασβεθῆναι, *at in corde meo tantum illius desiderium Ecclesiarum pacificandarum accensum esse affirmo ut vita mea libentissime redemptum velim illud odii incendum & invidiæ quod nequam ille spiritus concitavit extinctum penitus consapitumque esse.*

The Doxology Approven.

As Love, Humility, and Meekness are fit Graces in the Strong, for helping the Weak, so is also heavenly Wisdom, which is peaceable, gentle and easie to be intreated, *Jam.* 3. 17. and courteousness; 1 *Pet.* 5. 8. so that the strong Christian who is endowed with these Graces; instead of aggraging the sins of infirmity of the Weak, he will rather excuse them *in tanto* for their Ignorance, as *Peter* does the *Jews*, *Acts* 3. 17. and *Joseph* his Brethren, *Gen.* 50. 20. Secondly, He will bear with the froward Speeches of the Weak, as the Lord does with *Jonah*, chap. 4. verf. 9. *For he that covereth a transgression seeketh love*, Prov. 17. 9. yea, *Love covereth all sins*, Prov. 10. 22. to wit, of Infirmity. Thirdly, They will answer the froward words of the Weak with Meekness, for *a soft tongue breaketh the bone*, Prov. 25. 15. *Eli* in his imprudent rashness did mistake holy *Hannah*, 1 Sam. 1. 14. by her soft and humble answer *Elies* mistaken reproof was instantly turned into a prophetical blessing of her, which the Lord fulfilled.

This Duty of the Strongs bearing with the Infirmities of the Weak, must always be subordinate to our pleasing of God, which two are very well consistent; for our Saviour (and so should every good Christian) increased in favour with God and Man, *Luke*, 2. 52.

The Babes and Lambs of Christ must be ranked in two sorts, First, Some weak in Knowledge, but not so weak in sanctifying Grace; others, some more Knowledge, but less sanctifying Grace, and accordingly the strong should carry toward them; but they will find it much easier and sweeter to converse with these weak ones, who have some measure of Sanctification, though their Knowledge be weak, and these weak ones again must be subdivided, some only Weak; some both Weak and Sick, that is, not only weak in Knowledge, but also Sick by reason of Desertion, or Soul perplexities, tending to Despair; these, of all the weak Lambs, must be, and should be most tenderly dealt with, and of these especially our Saviour speaks in His Gospel, better a Milnstone be hanged about his Neck, and he be drowned in the deep of the Sea, then he offend one of these little ones that believe in me: Be cautious to try out, and careful to oversee these Lambs by any others.

As for you that are Strong, because you are not all of one size, I confess the task of bearing with the Infirmities, and gaining of the Weak to require strong Shoulders, and the Graces abovementioned required in the Strong for that Duty proves no less: And therefore ye that are strong in Knowledge, but weak in Mortification and Sanctification, no doubt that task will be more difficult to you; and therefore my humble advice to you is, that If you find you are not sufficiently strong in Mortification and Patience as to bear with the Infirmities of them, beware of falling in reasoning or disputing with them, for that will make no Healing, but rather more Strife: But withall, I would charge you to make this choice, rather to bear with the weak Lambs then for

pleasing

pleasing of Men to bear too much with Sinners, which is a displeasing of God; and thou who will not stoop to bear with the infirmities of the Weak, does not thy Father in Heaven bear with thy infirmities and grosser sins? does not thy Neighbour, with whom thou converseth, bear with thee also? nay, he deserves not to be born with, or live in Christian Society who is so passionate and wrathful, that he will neither bear word or look, for in many things we sin all, especially in sins of infirmity; beware thou be not like *Job*'s Friends, who had some measure of Knowledge, and came with real purpose to comfort their Friend, but for want of Charity they proved miserable Comforters, and instead of binding up his Soul wounds, ranckled them more.

As for you who are strong both in Knowledge and Grace, though the task be hard and difficult sometime to the strongest Christian, as upon this account sometimes ye will have to do with a Lamb so weak in Knowledge, that they will think you scarce deserve the name of Christian, or that you have Grace, or are walking in the way to Heaven; the best confutation of these, is to live with them, and before them in all good Conscience, and by time they will be convinced of their Error towards you.

As for you who are prophane in your Lives, and yet have more Knowledge in Religion then the weak Lambs, beware you take it not upon you to reproach these Lambs, for in so doing you serve the Devil, ye break the heart of the tender Lambs, ye grieve the Spirit of God; and who gave you authority to insult over them, or to do these Lambs any good to their Soul condition, thou has no Grace to do it, be ye a slave to Satan and his Lusts thy self; beware of the curse of *Amalek*, 1 *Sam.* 13. 3. his name to be blotted out from under Heaven, because with a cruel heart he pursued and smote the hindmost, feeble, faint and weary of *Israel*; and *Ezek* 34. 20. 21. because the strong Cattel thrust with side and shoulder, and push'd all the diseased with their horns, therefore will I destroy the fat, and the strong, I will feed them with judgment, I will seek that which was lost, bring again that which was driven away, bind up that which was broken, strengthen that which was sick.

As for you Lambs, when you consider all this care that your Heavenly Father takes of you, draw not hence this weak conclusion, That because your Father in Heaven commands the Strong to bear with your Infirmities, and to please you, for your good to Edification, do not overween upon that, as if your Father in Heaven loved you better then the Strong Christian, know you not, that the Father on Earth, when he hath a young tender Child very sick, or in danger of Death, he will command his elder Brother, who is yet more beloved of the Father, then that young Child, yet he will command him to sit up in the night, and attend his sick Brother, forbid him to speak a word to offend him,

why

this thankfull meeting, to wit, which any Strong Christian accosts thee in Christian love, to gain thee from thy Errours, to render the Information, and Instruction, beware thou reject not such a Messenger, Commissionated from thy Father, but with all Meeknefs and Gentleness lend thy Ear, and thy Heart to found Instruction; and if thou wilt keep Church Communion, and live orderly, thy Heavenly Father will more and more clear thee of thy doubts, and miftakes, and resolve to follow the advise of the Apostle, *Philip.* 3. 16. Which comes to this, that seing thy Neighbour Christian, and you agree in the Fundamentals, and saving Truths of Religion, to wit, one Catechism, and Confession of Faith, which are the compleat Rule to lead you both to Heaven, walk joyntly together in that way of Faith, and Holy Life; and for any other difference in opinion, till ye be cleared of your doubts, there is no danger for your Soul to let them lye asleep.

And for you that are Strong, remember that Precious Promise, In the Covenant of Grace, *Their sin I will remember no more,* Heb. 8. 12. *And none of his sins that he hath committed shall be mentioned unto him,* Ezek. 18. 22. and 33. 16. So in this be ye followers of God as dear Children, *Ephef.* 5. 1. Therefore I charge you, that their bygone escapes be mentioned no more, as you would have your Heavenly Father keep that Covenant of Grace to you, In the day of your accounts, therefore let an Act of Oblivion, in the Souls of the Strong in Gifts and Grace be passed, In favours of the Weak, who have returned, or are in the way of returning to the Bofom of their Mother Church, that so these Weak Lambs reflecting with an holy, and Inward Indignation against themselves, for their bygone Miftakes, and Wandrings, may rejoyce in the Lord, for the kindnefs, and Christian Brotherly Love, Humanity and Acceptance that they find, even from these whom before they looked upon, during their feparation as caftawayes, and and now they find that Truth confirmed, *Charity fuffereth long, and is kind*; all which Christian Kindnefle they finding in you, who are Strong, it may prove a strong Convincing and Gaining Argument upon their Spirits, that you have been, and are still in the Right Way to Heaven; *For by this shall all men know that ye are my difciples, if ye love one another,* John 13. 35 *And he that dwells in love, dwells in God, and God in him.* 1 Johu 4. 16.

And for you, beloved in the Lord, who through the good hand of God upon you, are returned to your Mother Church, to Communion in Word and Sacraments, let there be no Schifm in your Worfhip,

their God; shall your loving Mother Church receive you again in her bosome, and will ye be unthanktull and grieve her Soul, in retaining that halt which ye learned straying on the Mountains, and retain still to be a scandall to your Brethren, and a grief to her that bare you, God forbid.

As the Lords Covenant with *Noah*, and with mankind in him, and Sealled it with a visible Sign, to continue to all Generations, that he would not any more destroy the earth with a flood, and according to that Covenant hath iterat His Promise; *I have placed the sand so the bound of the sea, by a perpetuall decree, that it cannot passe it*, and though the waves tosse themselves, yet cannot it prevail though they roar, yet they cannot passe over it; I beseech the Lord, if it be His will that such another Inundation of Errours, with such Confusion, and disorder never overrun these three Kingdoms again, untill that day that the Lord send forth His Angells, and gather out of His Kingdom all things that offend, and the King shall seperat the Sheep from the Goats, and there shall be perfect Union, in singing one Song, with one Heart and Mouth unto all Eternity, To Him that sits upon the Throne, and to the Lamb, and to the Holy Ghost, be Glory and Praise, and shall be Glory and Praise, by all glorified Angels and Saints world without End. *A M E N.*

FINIS.

www.ingramcontent.com/pod-product-compliance
Lightning Source LLC
Chambersburg PA
CBHW022139160426
43197CB00009B/1358